The Ontario Cottage

The Ontario Cottage
Perfect of Its Kind

Lynne D. DiStefano and Dan Schneider

Photographs by
Steven Evans

Illustrations by
Ho Yin Lee

Vancouver / Toronto / Berkeley

To Ontario's Municipal Heritage Committees, whose advocacy and hard work has helped identify and protect so many of Ontario's places of heritage value. And to Architectural Conservancy Ontario, which assisted in the realization of this book.

Copyright © 2025 by Lynne D. DiStefano

25 26 27 28 29   5 4 3 2 1

All rights reserved, including those for text and data mining, artificial intelligence training, and similar technologies. No part of this book may be reproduced, stored in a retrieval system or transmitted, in any form or by any means, without the publisher's prior written consent or a license from Access Copyright.

Cataloguing data is available from Library and Archives Canada
ISBN 978-1-77327-274-0 (pbk.)

Design by Jessica Sullivan | DSGN Dept.
Photography by Steven Evans unless otherwise noted
Illustrations by Ho Yin Lee

Editing by Judy Phillips
Proofreading by Stephanie Fysh
Indexing by Emily LeGrand

Cover photographs by Steven Evans

Printed and bound in China by Shenzhen Reliance Printing Co., Ltd.

Figure 1 Publishing Inc.
Vancouver BC Canada
www.figure1publishing.com

Figure 1 Publishing is located in the traditional, unceded territory of the xʷməθkʷəy̓əm (Musqueam), Sḵwx̱wú7mesh (Squamish), and səlilwətaɬ (Tsleil-Waututh) peoples.

The authors wish to acknowledge that what is now known as Ontario is part of the traditional territory of Indigenous nations. We honour the ancestral guardians of its lands and waterways: the Anishinaabe, the Haudenosaunee Confederacy, the Wendat, and the Attiwonderonk. Today many Indigenous peoples continue to call this land home and act as its stewards; this responsibility extends to all of us: to share and care for the land for generations to come.

CONTENTS

Preface 6
Introduction 8

1 **Defining the Ontario Cottage** 10

2 **A Bird's-Eye View** 30

3 **Tradition and Style** 44

4 **Design Sources** 68

5 **As Good as Gold, or A Matter of Proportion** 80

6 **Constructing the Ontario Cottage** 92

7 **The Hipped Roof** 122

8 **The Veranda** 130

9 **Inside** 155

10 **Inhabiting the Ontario Cottage** 170

Conclusion 180

ACKNOWLEDGEMENTS 182
CONTRIBUTORS 184
NOTES 186
INDEX 195

PREFACE

I WAS FIRST DRAWN to the Ontario Cottage while working on an exhibition and book with historian and built heritage consultant Nancy Z. Tausky in the 1980s. Our research focused on a Southwestern Ontario architectural firm that designed a range of building types, including the cottage. As an upstart from south of the border, I wanted to know more about this unusual—to me—houseform. It intrigued me.

The first opportunity I had to start my cottage "journey" was when I was a student in the late 1980s at the Institute of Advanced Architectural Studies at the University of York (UK). For a required presentation, I focused on possible design sources for the Ontario Cottage and looked at architectural pattern books at the RIBA Library (British Architectural Library) in London and the University of York, as well as at emigrant guides at the British Library.

Inspired by my research findings, in the 1990s—in anticipation of a proposed exhibition at Museum London—I applied for and received a grant to identify representative Ontario Cottages. The resources I consulted included the Canadian Inventory of Historic Building and Local Architectural Conservation Advisory Committee (LACAC) databases, as well as colleagues, local contacts, and relevant primary and secondary sources, among them those at Archives of Ontario, Archives and Special Collections at Western University, Library and Archives Canada, and Special Collections at the Toronto Reference Library. Municipal heritage lists, in particular, were critical to the research process, as they indicated cottages within communities that are recognized for their architectural and/or historical values. With this information, I chose representative cottages that addressed broader aspects of the houseform in Ontario, as well as cottages that illustrated local building traditions and materials. Fieldwork confirmed the selection, and study photographs were shared with my photographer in preparation for the exhibition—and in expectation of an illustrated book to follow.

The exhibition *The Ontario Cottage: Perfect of Its Kind* opened in late 2000 at Museum London, with photographs by Steven Evans and drawings by Ho Yin Lee. A brochure was produced for the exhibition, but the promised book was delayed by my departure to Hong Kong, where my husband was working and where I had the opportunity to help set up a graduate program in architectural conservation at the University of Hong Kong.

Over two decades later, back in Ontario and with ongoing nudges from Ontario Cottage owners and those who love them, I returned to the long-postponed book project with fresh eyes and a deeper understanding of the importance of the Ontario Cottage. But it is only with the help and support of Dan Schneider (one of the nudgers and my co-author), the ongoing commitment and support of Steven Evans and Ho Yin Lee, and financial support from friends that the project was completed at last.

This book, *The Ontario Cottage: Perfect of Its Kind*, is our shared tribute to a distinctive layer of Ontario's cultural landscape and those who treasure it.

LYNNE D. DISTEFANO
Toronto
November 2024

INTRODUCTION

DOTTED ACROSS THE COUNTRYSIDE and clustered in towns and cities throughout the southern part of its namesake province, the Ontario Cottage is an almost ubiquitous presence. Like an old coat with which we have grown comfortable, the Ontario Cottage is taken for granted by Ontarians and claimed as our own. But it wasn't until 1963 that the Ontario Cottage was actually christened as such, by the renowned and formidable pair of architectural historians Marion MacRae and Anthony Adamson. In their seminal *The Ancestral Roof: Domestic Architecture of Upper Canada*, they identify it as one of the distinctive types of domestic architecture in the province.

What is the Ontario Cottage? In its basic configuration it resembles a child's crayon sketch of a house—a one-storey, hipped-roof building with a door placed squarely in the centre and a window placed on either side. This is the classic three-bay Ontario Cottage. But as we will see, the cottage can take sundry guises.

To many observers, what is most striking about a typical Ontario Cottage is its perfectly symmetrical facade. Arranged around the main doorway at the centre of the composition are matching or connecting elements to the right and left: the windows; the ends (or corners) of the walls; the horizontal band of the projecting eaves, sometimes broken by a small gable; the converging upward slopes of the roof; the ridgeline of the roof; and, often, the chimneys jutting up from the roof edge. In many Ontario Cottages, the side and even rear facades are also symmetrical. Because the walls of the house are all the same height, unlike with gable-roofed buildings, the effect is of an almost temple-like simplicity and rationality, one heightened by good proportions. The exterior symmetry is often mirrored inside. The entrance leads into a central hall around which rooms are organized. In the simplest floor plan, there are four rooms, two on either side of the hall; an additional fifth room is sometimes found at the back of the hall, where there may also be a rear door lined up with the front one.

Who built the first Ontario Cottage? While there is no definitive answer to the question, we know it to be a type of building associated with Ontario's colonial roots. When the British military and settlers first came to Upper Canada in the late eighteenth and early nineteenth centuries, they naturally brought with them knowledge of housing forms familiar from home. Some brought more than memories and skills; they carried with them copies of pattern books that featured contemporary Georgian notions of architectural design. More than a few of these architectural pattern books included designs for utilitarian and more ornamental or picturesque cottages, often with hipped roofs, where the four sides of the roof meet at a ridge or point.

Once transplanted to Canadian soil, what we have come to know as the Ontario Cottage adapted well to the conditions of its new homeland and the aspirations of its owners and builders. It became a favourite of the province's early settler farmers, both the more well-to-do and those of humbler origins. It took hold too in small towns and larger centres—its versatility appealed to middle-class merchants and mill and factory workers alike. While retaining its basic form, the Ontario Cottage evolved over more than a century through local variations and a succession of architectural styles—from Regency through Gothic to Italianate and Queen Anne.

Important in defining the uniqueness of the province's cultural landscapes, the Ontario Cottage is a treasured part of the Canadian architectural tradition. As we look closely at our subject—its origins, history, design characteristics, construction, and adaptability—accounting for the perennial appeal of the Ontario Cottage infuses much of the story.

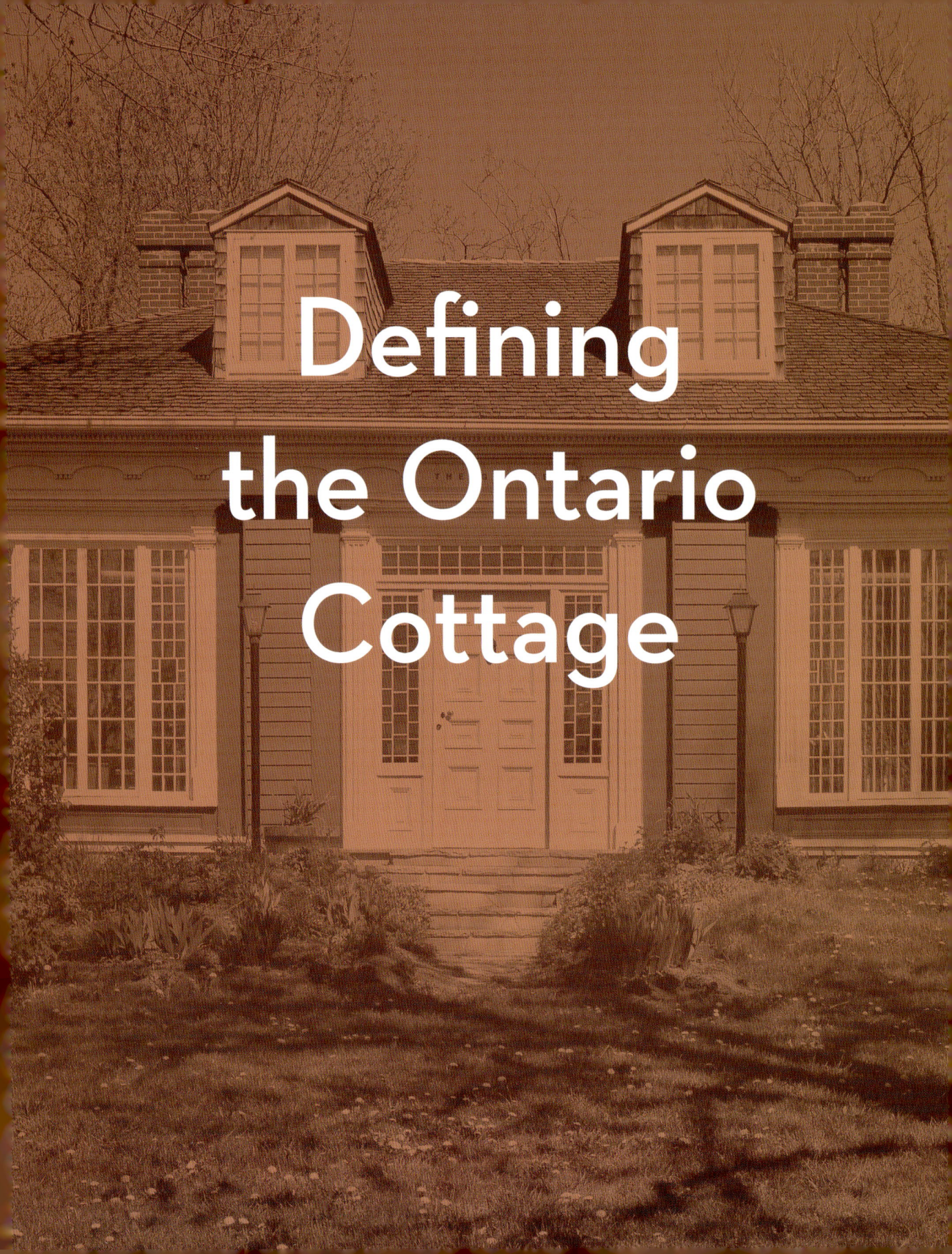

Defining the Ontario Cottage

1

A wise man, before commencing to build a house, will sit down and count the cost; he will ask himself, Where shall I build? What accommodation do I require? How much can I afford to lay out on my house? If his means are limited, he will attempt no ambitious imitation of a particular style, and will not impose upon the public with spurious examples of Italian or Gothic castles. No, he will endeavour to give a cheap cottage a tasteful and truthful appearance. He will have no showy ornaments and expensive carving on the exterior, while the interior is badly planned, meagre and poor. His cottage will be well planned and tastefully built, so that every part will bear the impress of refined judgment, and will afford quite as much pleasure in its way as a spacious mansion; although not the same kind of pleasure, it will be perfect of its kind.
FARM ARCHITECTURE, *Canada Farmer*, 1864

THIS CHARMING QUOTATION from the Farm Architecture column of the first (1864) issue of *The Canada Farmer* captures the sentiment at the heart of this book.[1] To be "perfect of its kind," a modest dwelling will provide a pleasing aesthetic based on human scale, good proportions, and a restrained use of decorative detail. An efficient floor plan and judicious use of materials (ideally local) complete the list. That the Ontario Cottage could meet these basic requirements so successfully and

1.1 Rose Cottage, 308 William Street, Oakville, 1856. This clapboard cottage with a shallow hipped roof, elegant entrance doorway, and double-hung windows is representative of earlier Ontario Cottages. The use of classical detailing for the entrance doorway reflects the influence of neoclassicism in Ontario during the early to mid-nineteenth century.
Photograph by Lynne D. DiStefano.

for so long is a tribute to its sound design and the good sense of its architects, builders, and owners.

In the evolution of Ontario's domestic architecture, the Ontario Cottage is one of a small number of distinctive imported—and then modified—houseforms; today, it is among the most recognizable in the province **(FIG. 1.1)**.[2] The Ontario Cottage is generally characterized as a one-storey, three-bay, hipped-roof building, though it is sometimes described as being a storey and a half. Its front elevation or facade is symmetrical, with a centrally placed entrance doorway and, typically, one window on either side (hence three openings or bays). Larger cottages may have two windows on either side (five bays). Deviations from the norm are not unusual.[3]

Importantly, the roof is hipped; unlike the simple two-sided gable roof, the roof slopes up gently on four sides to a point or ridge. At times, a small gable breaks the eaves above the front doorway. The exterior is graced by a porch or partial veranda at the front or a full veranda wrapping around the front and one or both sides. The floor plan may be symmetrical, at least for the main block of the building—a square or squarish rectangle.

Why does this seemingly modest house have such appeal? Where did it come from, and why did it endure? It is an intriguing story, not without complication.

Let's start with the term "cottage." The cottage as a type of English house was put forward by the British architecture scholar Ronald William Brunskill, who distinguishes between domestic vernacular buildings according to size.[4] He suggests four categories: Great House, Large House, Small House, and Cottage.[5] This approach has been expanded by numerous others, including Canadian cultural geographer Darrell A. Norris, who classifies the different types of detached houses found in Ontario before the Second World War based largely on the number of storeys and roof configuration. Norris's typology recognizes eight distinct pre-1939 houseforms. Of particular interest is the "1 Storey, Hip Roof" type identified by Norris, which describes the iconic form of the Ontario Cottage.[6]

Thomas F. McIlwraith in *Looking for Old Ontario: Two Centuries of Landscape Change* divides houses into only two categories: one-and-one-half storey and two storey. Year-round cottages are not included as a category, and when they are mentioned, they are called either a Regency Cottage or a Town Cottage.[7] On the other hand, MacRae and Adamson, in *The Ancestral Roof,* are clear about the cottage typology in Ontario. It was MacRae and Adamson—some sixty years ago—who first called what they referred to as a storey-and-a-half house with a hipped roof the "Ontario Cottage," arguing that this type of cottage is common in Ontario while rare in the northeastern United States.[8] The moniker stuck.

But names and classifications tell us only so much. Today in some parts of Canada,

1.2 Summer cottages, Port Ryerse, 1908. This cluster of wood-framed, hipped-roof cottages speaks to the versatility of the houseform. The four sides of the roof come to a point (Brunskill's "hipped roof on a projection"), a logical solution for small structures. Norfolk County Archives.

"cottage" is frequently used to describe a secondary residence, usually near a waterway, intended for seasonal use (FIG. 1.2),[9] though it can also connote a little house for year-round occupation. The historical meaning of the term is more complex.

In Great Britain, as early as the thirteenth century, a cottage was understood to be "a dwelling-house of small size and humble character."[10] As late as 1791, Walker's pronouncing dictionary defined a cottage as "a hut, a mean habitation" and a cottager as "one who dwells in a hut or cottage."[11] By the

1.3 Elizabeth Simcoe (1762–1850), *[A cottage] built by My brother Killaly 4 miles from London [Ontario]*, 1842, pencil on paper, 3⅝ × 3 inches. As a cottage orné, the building, which appears to be sited on the banks of the Thames River, is irregular in both silhouette and plan, and its triple-arch entrance porch, carved bargeboard, and window labels (hood moulds) recall medieval decorative and structural forms. The pillars of the entrance porch appear to be tree trunks, giving the cottage a touch of rusticity, a quality prized by proponents of the cottage orné. Elizabeth Simcoe loose sketches, F47-11-1-0-319, Thomas Fisher Rare Book Library, University of Toronto.

end of the eighteenth century, however, the term was being used by architects to describe a variety of houses offering a range of accommodation. From our present perspective, some of these "cottages" are certainly not modest either in scale or design character. The nineteenth-century Toronto architect John George Howard (1803–1890) went so far as to label one of his designs a "cottage villa," a seeming oxymoron.[12]

By the early nineteenth century, the term "cottage" was sometimes used interchangeably with "cottage orné," the French term for a more rustic—and decorative—cottage form. Strictly speaking, a cottage orné is one with picturesque qualities such as an irregular silhouette and stylistic attributes drawn from the medieval period. An example is seen in a nineteenth-century drawing from near London, Ontario (FIG. 1.3).

The cottage is sometimes also confused with the bungalow, a houseform with a distinct (but sometimes related) history. At the turn of the nineteenth century, in *Sketches for Country Houses, Villas, and Rural Dwellings*, the English-born Canadian architect John Plaw (1745–1820) featured a bungalow design described as "two Cottages ... with a Viranda in the manner of an Indian Bungalow" (FIG. 1.4).[13] This design for two semi-detached cottages refers to the hipped-roof houseform with a veranda that is indigenous to the Indian subcontinent, a form discussed further in chapter 8. The bungalow

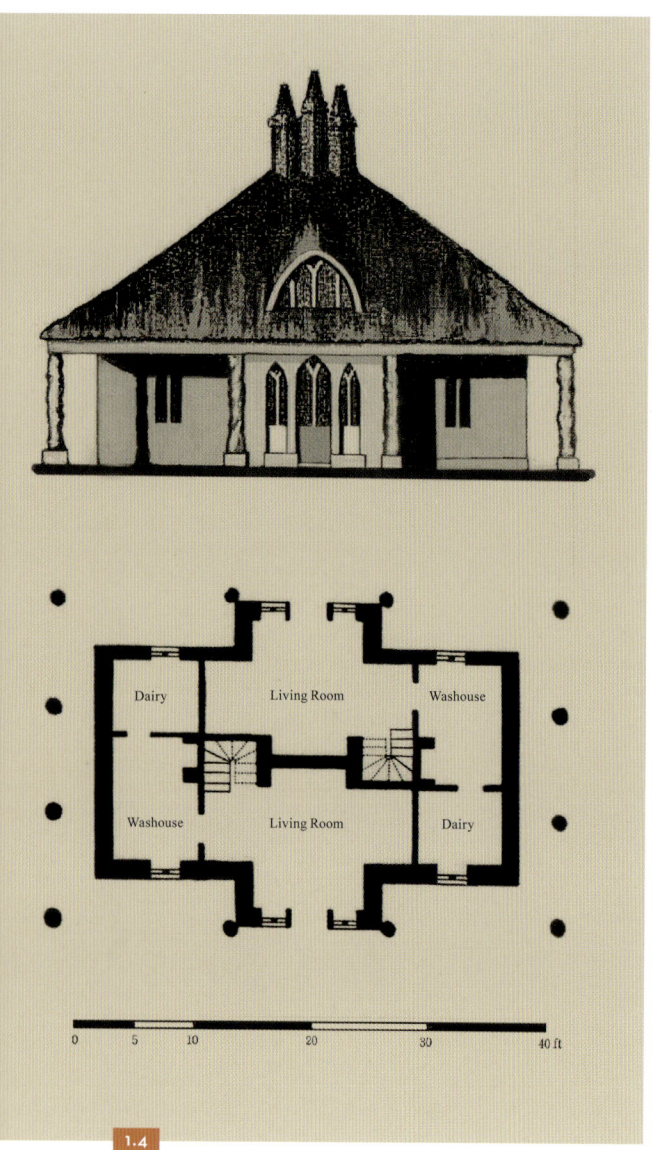

1.4 Plate VII: "...two cottages..., with a Viranda in the manner of an Indian Bungalow." In Plaw's elevation, a high-pitched hipped roof extends over a veranda that encircles all four sides of the building. The clever design positions the two cottage units back to back, rather than side by side as in a semi-detached houseform. Drawn by Ho Yin Lee after John Plaw, *Sketches for Country Houses, Villas, and Rural Dwellings [...]* (London: J. Taylor, 1800), 11, and plate VII.

as the North American house type we know today did not appear until the late nineteenth century. Although cottage-like in appearance, the North American bungalow has unique characteristics setting it apart from earlier British cottages, including Plaw's 1800 design.[14]

The Ontario Cottage, as an exemplar of the one- or one-and-a-half-storey house with a hipped roof, clearly has a long and complicated pedigree. But that the ostensibly humble cottage, as first described in medieval times,[15] could—with modification—come to provide homes for farmers and labourers, address the aspirations of a rising middle class, and even reflect the aesthetic interests of a society's upper echelon is remarkable.[16] That the cottage was "claimed" by different groups at different times speaks to its chameleon-like character and ongoing adaptability. Together, PLATES 1.1–1.12 provide a wide-ranging sample of the typology.

PLATE 1.1
Cruickston Farm

Cruickston Park Lane, Cambridge, n.d.

PLATE 1.2
James Lazier House

Prince Edward County,
near Green Point, c. 1840

PLATE 1.3

Johnson Cottage

Levi Street,
Port Bruce, n.d.

PLATE 1.4
Colborne Street, London, c. 1883 or earlier

PLATE 1.5

Vansittart Avenue,
Woodstock, 1855

PLATE 1.6
William Trick Cottage

Ridout Street,
Port Hope, c. 1850

PLATE 1.7
James Street,
Kingston, before 1850

PLATE 1.8

Whalen Road,
near Marysville, n.d.

PLATE 1.9
Dundas Street West,
Mississauga (Erindale), c. 1828

PLATE 1.10
Warner Road,
Niagara-on-the-Lake
(Village of St. Davids), 1837

PLATE 1.11

Kirkland Street,
Guelph, 1878 on the left, 1877 on the right

PLATE 1.12
Yates Street,
St. Catharines, before 1852

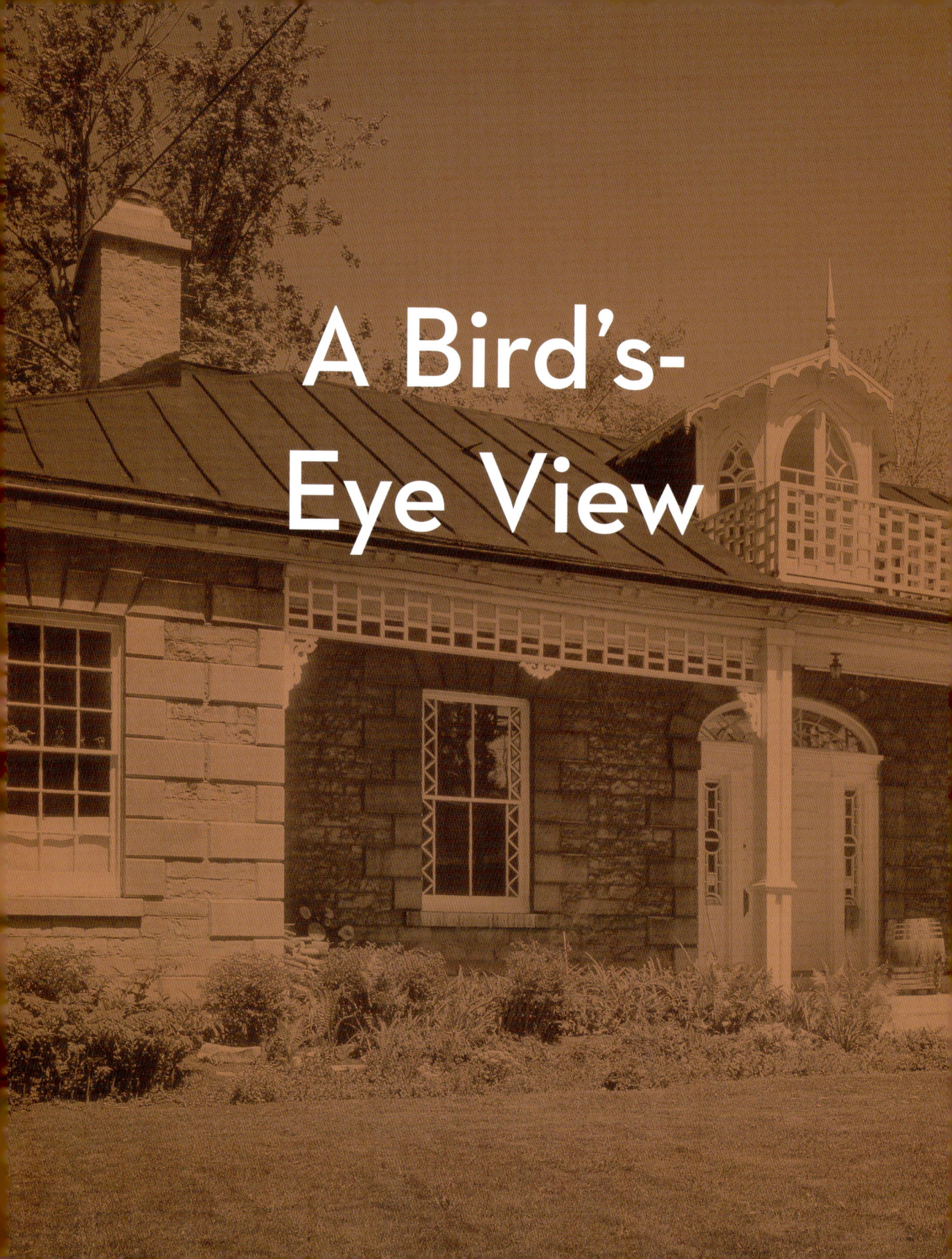

A Bird's-Eye View

2

> The territory that became the Province of Ontario in 1867 was dramatically different from the territory that had become the Province of Upper Canada in 1791. In most of southern Ontario, the virgin forest had been largely replaced by geometrically precise plots of cleared farmland. Five cities had more than ten thousand people each, and several others were approaching that mark.
> **RANDALL WHITE,** *Ontario, 1610–1985*

IF WE WERE TO GO BACK IN TIME and take a hot-air balloon ride over the cities and towns of Ontario in the late 1800s, we would spot hundreds upon hundreds of hipped-roof cottages—standing alone, in clusters, and even in row after row—all helping define an unfolding urban landscape. And as our balloon drifted over the province's countryside, we would espy the cottage again and again as a farmhouse in the domesticated rural landscape, often in picturesque settings.

Favoured by rural, suburban, and urban dwellers alike, the versatile cottage spread across much of the southern part of the province through the nineteenth century and into the twentieth.

In the early European settlements of today's Ontario (Upper Canada until 1841), hipped-roof cottages were already an established houseform. In Niagara-on-the-Lake (founded as Butlersburg and renamed Newark in 1792), Butler House, a five-bay, hipped-roof cottage in clapboard, was built in around

2.1 Sir James Edward Alexander (1803–1885), *Baron de Tuylls, Goderich, C.W.*, 1843, pen-and-ink with wash and watercolour over pencil, 3⅞ × 6¼ inches. Alexander Sketchbook, Folio 24, verso 22, Library and Archives Canada.

1817, shortly after the end of the War of 1812 and the withdrawal of American forces from the area (PLATE 2.1). In 1830, Baron de Tuylls, a Belgian nobleman, built—in "rough cast-on-log"—a five-bay, hipped-roof cottage with enviable views of the mouth of the Maitland River. (Nearby Goderich was founded in 1827.) The cottage no longer exists, but a drawing reveals its presence and setting (FIG. 2.1). In Kingston (founded by the French in 1673, destroyed by the British in 1758, and settled by Loyalists after 1783), Charles Place, an exceptional five-bay stone cottage with a recessed porch, or umbrage, was constructed in around 1830 (PLATES 2.2 + 2.3). In Woodstock (first settled in 1800), Drew Cottage was constructed in 1833 (PLATE 2.4), while in Toronto (founded in 1793 as York), a cottage called Drumsnab was built in around 1834 on the edge of what became Rosedale. Substantially modified, the latter building still exists; in its original form, it was a one-storey stone cottage with an extensive veranda (FIG. 8.3).

As the century wore on and the province was developed, hipped-roof cottages appear in places such as Port Hope, Brantford, London, and Stratford, as well as rural areas in between. To get a rough sense of the incidence of cottages across the southern tier of the province by the mid- to late nineteenth century, two sets of publications offer insight: Tremaine's county maps and Ontario's county atlases. The illustrated county maps were published by cartographer George Tremaine between 1856 and 1864, while the illustrated county atlases were primarily published between 1875 and 1881 by map and atlas publishers H. Belden & Co. The atlases in particular provide a good source of information about the spread of hipped-roof cottages in more rural locations.

Seven of the thirteen Tremaine county maps include images of hipped-roof cottages: six appear on the map of Oxford (which includes Woodstock); three on the map of Lincoln and Welland (which includes Niagara-on-the-Lake); another three on the map of Norfolk (which includes Simcoe); and one or two on the maps of Brant, Durham, Middlesex, and Peel. (There are no illustrations of hipped-roofed cottages on the maps of Halton, Prince Edward, and Waterloo Counties, and no illustrations of any kind of domestic building on the maps of Elgin, Ontario, and York Counties.)

Tremaine's county maps confirm that, by mid-century, a range of rural and urban cottages were a distinctive part of the cultural landscape in many counties. On the Oxford map (1857), for example, there is a stolid three-bay, hipped-roof cottage in a rural setting for Wm. C. McLeod and an expansive three-bay, hipped-roof urban cottage with a sweeping veranda for George Alexander. Both are in Woodstock. (See **PLATE 2.5** for a contemporary photograph of the latter.)

Later in the century, county atlases reflect the widespread appearance of hipped-roof cottages in rural settings.[1] Usually sketched from a bird's-eye view, these cottages are

RES. OF JOHN BRITTON CON. 7, LOT 7, HULLETT TP. ONT.

depicted in their (idealized) agricultural landscapes—fenced with formal gardens at the front and tidy orchards and expansive fields in the background, and with a clear segregation of outbuildings from the house (FIG. 2.2). The atlas for Northumberland and Durham Counties (which includes Port Hope and Cobourg) is illustrated with ten hipped-roof cottages, while that for Huron County to the west has four. Those for Elgin County, Frontenac County, Lennox and Addington County, Lincoln County, and Welland County are each illustrated with three; those for Hastings and Prince Edward Counties, Ontario County, and Perth County each have two; and those for Leeds and Grenville Counties and Peel County each have one.

Tremaine's maps indicate the presence of hipped-roof cottages in a range of rural and urban locations in the 1850s and 1860s, while

2.2 *Residence of John Britton.* From *Illustrated Historical Atlas of the County of Huron Ont.* (Toronto: H. Belden & Co., 1879), 68. Archives and Special Collections, Western Libraries.

county atlases record cottages primarily in rural settings during the 1870s and early 1880s. Starting about 1870, there was a shift as the demand for skilled tradesmen in urban centres created a corresponding demand for housing close to places of employment. Small suburban houses—cottages—satisfied this need. As observed in the *London Advertiser*'s City and Vicinity column in 1873,

> The suburbs on all sides of the city bear manifess [*sic*] indications of thrift among the inhabitants.... In many instances tradesmen and others have purchased lots in those localities, and built homes for themselves there.[2]

The article further notes that "there have not been so large a number of small houses erected this year within the city limits, owing to the fact that many tradesmen have been locating in the suburbs."[3]

As cities and towns developed—or further developed—local industries, especially in the late nineteenth and early twentieth centuries, the emerging factory workforce also required reasonably priced housing. The hipped-roof cottage was again an attractive option.

Take Brantford, where a wide range of cottages was built from the late 1820s right through to the early 1940s. Indeed, the Ontario Cottage became so common in the city that the local version is often referred to as the "Brantford Cottage." In the early twentieth century, in response to the need for affordable housing, a variant, the Diamond Cottage, appeared. The name refers to the shape of the window in the front gable (though the "diamond" can be seen more prosaically as a simple, but rotated, square window) **(PLATE 2.6)**. Unique to Brantford, these distinctive hipped-roof cottages are found near factory sites and along the city's rail lines **(PLATE 2.7)**.[4]

Why was the Ontario Cottage so popular a houseform throughout the province? What explains its persistence for over a century? In the next chapter, we start to unravel the secret of its appeal.

A Bird's-Eye View   35

PLATE 2.1
Butler House

Simcoe Street,
Niagara-on-the-Lake, c. 1817

PLATE 2.2
Charles Place
Lower Union Street, Kingston, c. 1830

PLATE 2.3
Charles Place
Lower Union Street, Kingston, c. 1830: detail

PLATE 2.4
Drew Cottage

Rathbourne Avenue, Woodstock, 1833

PLATE 2.5
Rokewood

Jack Poole Drive,
Woodstock, 1847

PLATE 2.6
Brighton Avenue, Brantford, c. 1906

PLATE 2.7

Usher Street, Brantford, 1910s

Tradition and Style

3

> The matured eye... regards, with unspeakable delight, the simple cottage.
>
> JAMES MALTON, *An Essay on British Cottage Architecture*, 1798

ANALYZING THE ONGOING APPEAL of the Ontario Cottage begins with searching out its underlying architectural form—and understanding the interaction of that form with a century-long parade of architectural styles.

PERSISTENCE OF THE CLASSICAL

The Ontario Cottage has a noble ancestry. Its most direct stylistic precedent is the Palladian style, a style that defined British architecture, especially domestic architecture, during the first half of the eighteenth century. This style is often referred to more generally as the Georgian style, as it was widespread during the reigns of the Hanoverian kings, George I, George II, George III, and George IV, from 1714 to 1830.

The Palladian label, by contrast, is more allusive, denoting a style of architectural expression developed almost two centuries earlier by the Italian Renaissance architect Andrea Palladio (1508–1580). Palladio's work, based on Roman classical architecture and influenced by his Italian contemporaries, had such an impact on British architecture that his name is practically synonymous with the architecture of the early Georgian period.[1]

3.1 Villa Emo, Fanzolo, near Castelfranco Veneto (Italy), c. 1564. Palladio's villas, in contrast to his palaces and public buildings, were built on agricultural sites. Villa Emo's main building block, with its entrance portico or frontispiece (temple-front), suggests a typical Ontario Cottage with a central gable, though the contrast in scale is considerable. The arcaded wings of the villa, which terminate in dovecotes, were used for functions related to farming. Drawn by Ho Yin Lee after illustration 55, book 2. Andrea Palladio, *The Four Books of Architecture*, trans. Robert Tavernor and Richard Schofield (Cambridge, MA: MIT Press, 1997).

At its essence, a Palladian building is one exhibiting such qualities as good (well-ordered) proportions, a harmonious arrangement of building parts, and axial symmetry, where one side of a building's main facade is the same as the other side.

Looking back to the classical world, we see these same qualities described in the first century BCE by Vitruvius, an influential Roman architect and engineer, in his *Ten Books on Architecture*. The ten-volume book, a comprehensive guide to architectural principles and building construction, was first published in Latin as *De architectura*. As Vitruvius writes in "The Fundamental Principles of Architecture," the second chapter of book 1, "Architecture depends on Order..., Arrangement..., Eurythmy, Symmetry, Propriety, and Economy."[2]

Although most of these concepts seem clear enough, Vitruvius goes on to define them at length. "Order" refers to understanding the parts of a building and their proportional relationship to the building as a whole, while "arrangement" refers to the placement of building parts with the intent of creating an "elegance of effect." Eurythmy, or "beauty and fitness," is achieved through the adjustment of building parts, and symmetry is the "proper agreement between the parts of a building as well as the relationship between the different parts and the building itself." "Propriety," more complex, refers to the perfection of a style based on recognized principles, the consistent or rational design of buildings, and/or the well-considered location or siting of buildings. Economy is a "thrifty balancing of cost and common sense" and the suitability of buildings for specific social classes.[3]

In the long era from the time of Vitruvius to the early fifteenth century, the influence of the classical world receded. With the rediscovery and documentation of classical ruins, especially Roman, during the Renaissance, *The Ten Books on Architecture* was also rediscovered. The book informed the work and writing of Andrea Palladio during the sixteenth century and, later, that of British architects such as Inigo Jones in the early seventeenth century and Colin Campbell and Richard Boyle, third Earl of Burlington, in the early eighteenth.[4]

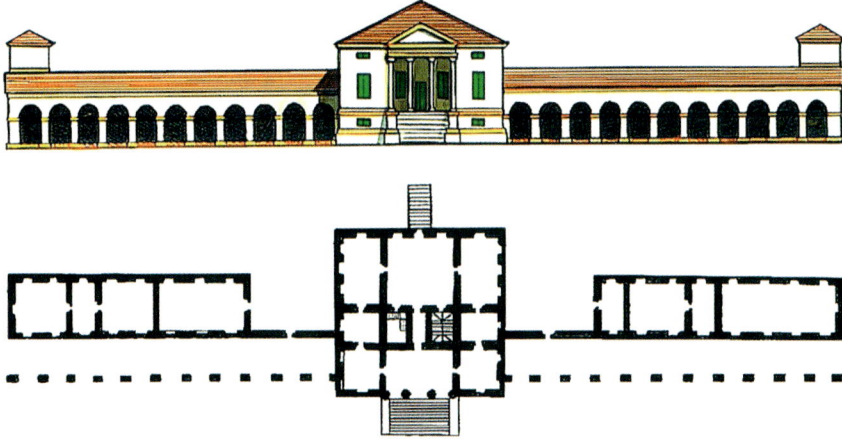

Palladio's writing on architectural design, *I quattro libri dell'architectura* (*The Four Books of Architecture*), is directly relevant to an understanding of the design of the Ontario Cottage. Palladio agreed with Vitruvius on the objectives of architecture (although, as the more practical of the two, in a different sequence: utility, durability, and beauty, rather than durability, utility, and beauty). He also shared Vitruvius's belief in the need for a sense of overall order, and a sense of relationship between building parts and their relationship to the building as a whole.[5] Later, in chapter 5, we look more closely at such relationships when considering the Ontario Cottage's proportions.

Palladio's detailed advice to architects is realized in his own work. In his buildings, the front facade is symmetrical and composed of a raised basement, prominent main floor, and functional attic. The main entrance is placed on the building's central axis (running through the middle of the facade), windows on either side of the entrance are identical, and those near the ends of the facade are set back from the building's corners. Inside, rooms on the main floor (the *piano nobile*) are symmetrically arranged around a central hall or the equivalent, the attic is used for storage, and the kitchen is relegated to the high basement. The overall composition of the front elevation tends to be horizontal in feel, with a central portico adding an element of focus.[6] A hipped roof contains the entire composition.

The portico is a major element in Palladian design. The classical portico, centrally placed, is "a roof supported by columns."[7] In Palladio's work, especially his designs for smaller houses, which he calls *villas*, the portico is sometimes flattened and treated more like a decorative frontispiece culminating in a triangular pediment, closed at the top and "breaking" the lower line of the roof (FIG. 3.1). In Palladio's words,

> In all the buildings for farms and also for some of those in the city I have built a tympanum [frontispiece] on the front facade where the principal doors are, because tympanums accentuate the entrance of the house and contribute greatly to the grandeur and magnificence of the building.... The ancients also employed them in their buildings.[8]

There is practical thinking behind this too, as roof runoff is redirected to the sides of the pediment, protecting the entrance.

Centuries later, we find Palladio's ideas reflected in Ontario architecture. The Ontario Cottage, in particular, exhibits many of the same qualities as the developed Palladian villa. Proportions, although simple, are well considered; building parts, especially the main door and front windows, are carefully distributed; and the main facade is symmetrical. The portico is also often seen, though almost always as a frontispiece in the form of a roof gable over a centrally placed main entrance. This retains the water-shedding function of Palladio's tympanum and serves as a focal point for the front elevation. Earlier Ontario examples of the frontispiece are more closely aligned with Palladian proportions, whereas later examples reflect the verticality associated with Gothic styles—or perhaps simply the restrictions posed by narrow lots and small budgets.

While at first a path of direct influence may be hard to discern, the spirit of Palladio is seen in the cottage designs found in a guidebook produced specifically for Scottish settlers in Ontario (FIG. 3.2).

Given the long Georgian period (1714–1830), it is not surprising that the Palladian style had other "contenders" over time, even if many of the new design expressions also reached back to classical architecture. We see a refinement of Palladian ideas—flatter, more linear architectural treatment based in part on newly discovered Greek architectural remains—and sometimes an awkward imitation of classical Greek forms, especially the temple (FIG. 3.3). This complex period of architectural expression at the end

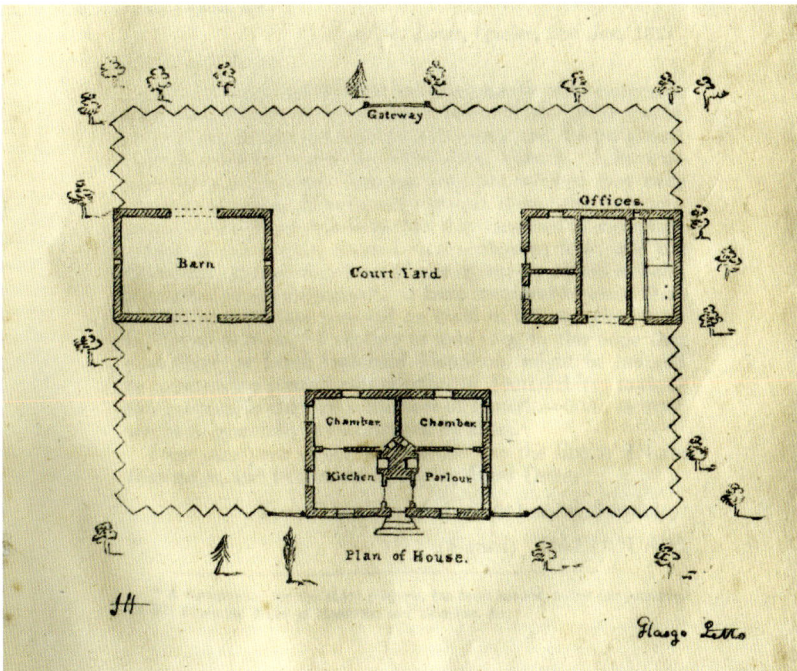

3.2 This design, one of nine in Lamond's *Narrative*, is influenced by the three-part design of one type of Palladian villa. The centre building is the "house," the set-backed building to the right contains the "offices," and the set-backed building to the left is the "barn." All three have hipped roofs, two with matching entrance porticoes and one with a massive central chimney as its focal point. Most of Lamond's other designs, which are small cottages without implied wings, likely reflect the lingering influence of Palladio as well. We'll return to this series of illustrations in chapter 4. Design 9. In Robert Lamond, *A Narrative of the Rise & Progress of Emigration, from the Counties of Lanark & Renfrew, to the New Settlements in Upper Canada, on Government Grant [...]* (Glasgow: Chalmers & Collins, 1821), inset between 68 and 69.

of the Georgian period and bleeding into the Victorian is known as neoclassicism.[9]

The more linear interpretation of classical forms is especially germane to our understanding of the design of some of Ontario's earliest and finest hipped-roof cottages. These buildings are frequently labelled "Regency Cottages" (referencing the future George IV acting as regent for the incapacitated George III in the decade 1810–20). Regency Cottages tend to be lower to the ground, less "boxy" in form, and with distinctive decorative features such as recessed arches in low relief. (See FIG. 4.3 for an example.)

Tradition and Style

3.3 Elizabeth Simcoe (1782–1850), *Castle Frank…*, 1796, watercolour on paper, 17½ × 11 inches. The front porch of the Simcoes' summer home is a rustic version of a Greek temple portico. Such literalism is seldom seen in the Ontario Cottage, but the porch reminds us that Palladio's portico or frontispiece, later transposed as the front gable of many Ontario Cottages, was inspired by the classical temple. Elizabeth Simcoe loose sketches, F 47-11-1-0-231, Thomas Fisher Rare Book Library, University of Toronto.

APPEAL OF THE GOTHIC

Alongside contemporary architects' fascination with the Greco-Roman, the Georgian period witnessed an increasing interest in medieval architecture, especially architecture of the Gothic style. Great Britain's castles and ecclesiastical buildings from the Middle Ages were a ready source of ideas. Rather confusingly, what we call British Gothic architecture evolved over a number of centuries and is categorized into three distinct phases, all of which depend on the pointed arch form: Early English, Decorated, and Perpendicular. The Early English phase (c. 1180 to c. 1280) is known for its narrow (lancet) windows that usually lack tracery;[10] the Decorated phase (c. 1280 to after 1350), for exuberant decoration and tracery; and the Perpendicular phase (c. 1350–1550), for a vertical emphasis in decorative details and structure.[11]

Building qualities such as verticality were explored, especially in the design of public buildings, near the end of the Georgian period. However, for domestic buildings, references to the Gothic are generally found in details like pointed arches for the tops of doorways and windows, as well as such decorative details as trefoils and quatrefoils (three- and four-lobed motifs). The latter were sometimes adapted as window frames or tucked into corners created by arches within rectangular or square openings for doors or windows. Popular too

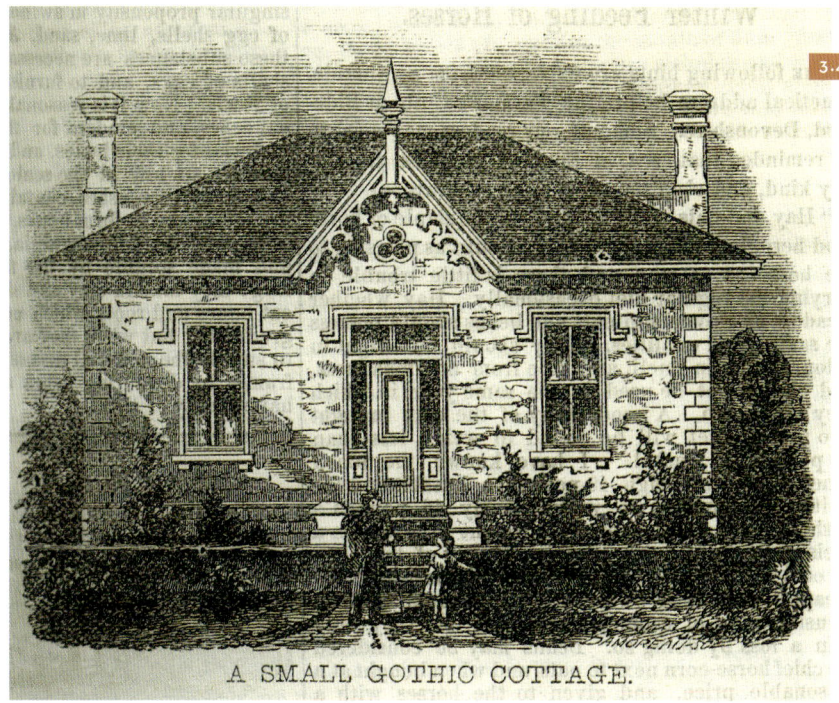

3.4 "A Small Gothic Cottage," *Canada Farmer* 1, no. 2 (February 1, 1864): 21. This illustration is one of two in this edition's Farm Architecture column. The other illustration, "A Log House," speaks to a simpler housing solution with its gable roof, though the reader is told that the house "can be made tasteful, and even ornamental, by raising a small gable over the [centrally placed] front door" (20). Archives and Special Collections, Western Libraries.

were carved bargeboards for gables and carved or turned finials to terminate gables. Such decorative uses of the Gothic vocabulary were actually employed in domestic buildings during the latter part of the eighteenth century, well before the more archaeological approach to the replication of the style.

The Ontario Cottage—essentially a Palladian houseform—is sometimes enlivened with Gothic detail. In the elevation for the Small Gothic Cottage, as published in *The Canada Farmer*, the stolid symmetrical facade is "Gothicized" by a front gable enclosing a trefoil-shaped window **(FIG. 3.4)**, the gable's carved bargeboard, and the gable apex supporting a robust finial.[12] The door and front windows are capped by flat (or perpendicular) arches, associated with Gothic's Perpendicular phase.

But remove the Gothic trappings and we are left with a classic self-contained form that can be "dressed up" with details from any number of styles.

CLASSICAL AND GOTHIC—AND BEYOND

The fascination with the classical, both Greek and Roman, and the Gothic continues into the reign of Victoria (1837–1901). The relationship between the two styles was sometimes one of rivals, leading to what has even been called a "Battle of the Styles" among their supporters. In reality, it was less a battle and more an uneven transition in architectural inspiration from Greek and Roman classical sources to British and European medieval ones.

The "battle" played out slowly across Ontario. The Fountain Street South cottage (c. 1850) in the (now) Cambridge community of Preston, with its striking portico supported by both Doric and square columns, and an entablature with regularly placed motifs based on the Greek key, shows an impressive adaptation of Palladian-inspired design (PLATE 3.1); while Rose Cottage (1856) in Oakville offers a more subtle reference to classical forms, as seen in its simple yet elegant neoclassical doorway with a rectangular transom divided by vertical muntins (PLATES 3.2 + 3.3). Gothic references emerge later and can be found in multiple cottages across the southern tier of the province, especially between London and Port Hope, as in Carfrae Cottage (c. 1860) in London (PLATE 3.4) and our now familiar Small Gothic Cottage from 1864. The details are secondary to the form but provide nonetheless an evocative frosting.[13]

By the mid-nineteenth century, other—and more eclectic—Victorian styles are increasingly evident. The Italianate, whose lineage can be traced to the Italian Renaissance and ultimately to Roman classical forms and details, is especially popular. In cottages, the style is seen in a preference for round and/or segmental arches over door and window openings, and for decorative brackets at the eaves, as in the Main Street North cottage (1858) in Bayfield (PLATE 3.5). The Romanesque Revival, which refers to the use of Roman forms and details during the medieval period, appears later and features round-arch window openings, as in the Douro Street cottage (1896) in Stratford (PLATE 3.6).

High Victorian Gothic, also called Picturesque Eclecticism, made its appearance by the 1870s.[14] This eclectic style can be puzzling in the complexity of its formal and decorative elements, but the small scale of most cottages limits the extent of its application. The Albion Street cottages in Brantford (PLATE 3.7; 1872 on the left, 1874 on the right) successfully combine numerous styles (neoclassical, Gothic, and Italianate) with an effective use of bichromatic brickwork to highlight such building elements as segmental window arches, panels below the front windows (on the right only), and end quoins. The main floors are set off from the basement through the use of bichromatic brickwork. Other examples of bichromatic brickwork are seen in the Beech Street cottage (1889) in Collingwood (PLATE 3.8), the Barry Avenue cottage (c. 1860) in Mississauga (PLATE 3.9), and the Mornington Street cottage (1863) in Stratford (PLATE 3.10).

Toward the end of the century, cottage design is influenced by Queen Anne Revival. This misnamed style, like High Victorian Gothic, is based on an eclectic mixture of historical antecedents—in this case, fifteenth-century country-house and cottage Elizabethan architecture, a blend of medieval and classical motifs—and is described as being "varied, colourful, and light-hearted."[15] In Aylmer, there is a striking Ontario Cottage (1887) with a unique corner tower, a signature attribute of the style (PLATE 3.11). The building can best be seen as an imaginative amalgam of High Victorian Gothic and Queen Anne Revival. Its name, Swiss Cottage, only adds to its charm.

The Aylmer cottage, in its use of a corner tower, represents one of the more notable exceptions to the usual Ontario Cottage profile. Another is the introduction of bay windows, a further Queen Anne attribute, which also break the flat, contained wall surface of the houseform, as seen in a cottage (early 1880s) in St. Thomas (PLATE 3.12). Fortunately, perhaps, the small scale of the Ontario Cottage (along with the control imposed by a hipped roof) prevents an excess of High and Late Victorian exuberance.

Could it be the interplay between stylistic details and the underlying Palladian houseform that explains the Ontario Cottage's special character? As J.C. Loudon, a nineteenth-century landscape architect and writer who we meet in the next chapter, astutely observed, the slight "allusion" to a well-known style "operates upon the imagination and at once gives the idea of style."[16] When such allusion is married to a "classical" form of sound proportions and enduring appeal, we begin to understand the lure of the hipped-roof cottage.

PLATE 3.1
Fountain Street South,
Cambridge (Preston), c. 1850

PLATE 3.2
Rose Cottage

William Street, Oakville, 1856

PLATE 3.3
Rose Cottage

William Street, Oakville, 1856: detail

PLATE 3.4
Carfrae Cottage

Carfrae Street,
London, c. 1860

PLATE 3.5
Main Street North, Bayfield, 1858

PLATE 3.6
Douro Street, Stratford, 1896

PLATE 3.7
Albion Street, Brantford,
1872 on the left, 1874 on the right

PLATE 3.8
Beech Street,
Collingwood, 1889

PLATE 3.9
Barry Avenue,
Mississauga (Streetsville), c. 1860

PLATE 3.10
Mornington Street, Stratford, 1863

PLATE 3.11

Swiss Cottage

Talbot Street West, Alymer, 1887

PLATE 3.12

St. Thomas,
early 1880s

Design Sources

4

> I have been examining all the plans for cottages in Loudon's book, and picked out what seem the best things. Oh, what a happiness it would be to set the pattern about here! I think, instead of Lazarus at the gate,[1] we should put the pig-sty cottages outside the park-gate.
>
> GEORGE ELIOT, *Middlemarch*, 1871

UNDERSTANDING THE ONTARIO COTTAGE from a tradition and style perspective is one thing; explaining its appearance in the province is another. While it is clear that the Ontario Cottage is of British derivation, what are the sources of its design and how did it come to Ontario?

Part of the answer lies with the architectural pattern book.[2] From the late eighteenth century until well into the nineteenth, British architectural pattern books—handsome publications containing building designs and plans, usually prepared by architects—reflected an interest in cottage designs and promoted their use. Some of the earliest architectural pattern books, those from the late 1700s, address the dismal housing conditions of farm labourers and offer a range of low-cost cottage options. At the same time, the cottage starts to be viewed more broadly as an attractive housing choice for a rising middle class, including its use as lodges on country estates (FIG. 4.1).[3]

One of the most influential examples of architectural pattern books during this period is Scottish landscape architect J.C. Loudon's *Encyclopaedia of Cottage, Farm,*

4.1 Gate Lodge, Kinoith, Shanagarry, County Cork, Republic of Ireland, n.d. This compact gate lodge in stone has a pyramidal hipped roof that rises to a central chimney.[4] The facade is plain except for stone perpendicular arches over paired front windows. Photograph by Lynne D. DiStefano.

and Villa Architecture and Furniture, first published in 1833.[5] This ambitious publication, with its more than two thousand engravings, was widely circulated in Great Britain, especially among the middle class. It clearly made an impression: in the epigraph that opens this chapter, from George Eliot's 1871 *Middlemarch*, an epic novel about English provincial life, young Dorothea Brooke, one of the main characters, is conversing with a local estate owner about "Loudon's book."

Pattern books and emigrant guides—and the cottage designs they touted—made their way, along with emigrant populations, to other parts of the British Empire, including Ontario, then known as Upper Canada. Although there is limited documentation linking the Ontario Cottage with a *specific* design source (apart from one emigrant guide, discussed below), it is revealing to chart the development of ideas and designs for cottages in different parts of Great Britain and trace their eventual migration to Upper Canada.

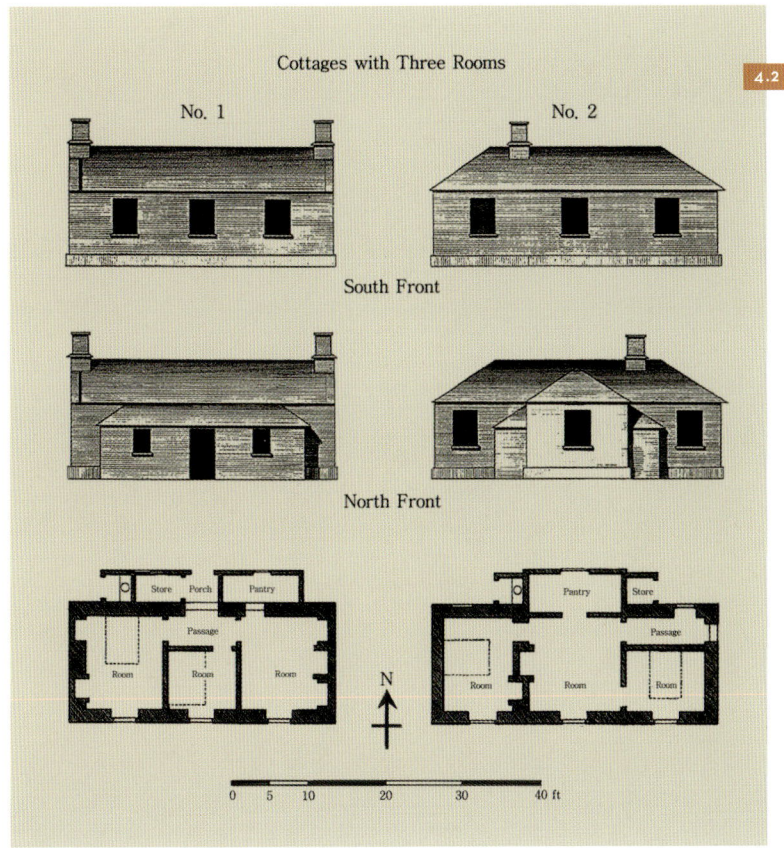

4.2 Plate XII: *Cottages with Three Rooms*. Number 1 is a three-bay, gable-roof cottage with an enclosed, centrally placed entrance; and Number 2, a three-bay, hipped-roof cottage with an entrance placed at the side. The asymmetrical placement of the entrance is unusual, but it does not detract from the rigid symmetry of the front and rear elevations. This second design is significant, as it appears to be the earliest design in architectural pattern books for a one-storey, three-bay cottage with a hipped roof. Drawn by Ho Yin Lee after John Wood, *A Series of Plans for Cottages or Habitations of the Labourer [. . .]*, rev. ed. (London: Architectural Library, 1806), n.p.

SPREAD OF THE ARCHITECTURAL PATTERN BOOK

The first architectural pattern book is John Wood's *A Series of Plans for Cottages or Habitations of the Labourer*, published in England in 1781, almost a decade before architectural pattern books became popular there.[6] In this early effort to address the appalling housing conditions of the poor, Wood offers a series of cottage designs that vary by the number of rooms (one to four) and the type of roof (gable or hipped). The design most relevant for our purposes is seen in his plate XII, which shows two three-room cottages, one with a hipped roof (FIG. 4.2).[7]

In Ireland, under the patronage of the Farming Society of Ireland, architect William Barber published what is most likely the first Irish architectural pattern book, *Farm Buildings* (after 1802), to promote "a regular system of rural building." He recommended his book "to the consideration of the man of

4.3 Design X; plate XIII: *Plan of a Farm House and Offices.* This elegant three-bay cottage was intended to be seen from the "high road." With its paired chimneys, low-pitched hipped roof, and shallow recessed arches, it displays the primary attributes of a Regency Cottage. Note too that the cottage sits low to the ground, another attribute of the style and different from Scottish examples. Drawn by Ho Yin Lee after Arthur C. Taylor, *Designs for Agricultural Buildings Suited to Irish Estates [. . .]* (Dublin: Grant and Bolton, 1841), n.p.

taste, whose eye seeks for gratification; and to the man of feeling, whose heart delights in the comfort and enjoyment of his neighbours or his tenantry."[8] Included among Barber's designs is one for a labourer's single cottage, a small three-bay, hipped-roof cottage.[9]

Later, Arthur C. Taylor observes in his 1841 book, *Designs for Agricultural Buildings Suited to Irish Estates,*

> Many proprietors have given encouragement to their tenantry to build houses, etc., by granting leases and giving in part materials, etc.; but that as there exist no model plans suited to this country to erect from, these houses have been generally very defective in construction, and deficient in accommodation and convenience.[10]

Among the designs featured in Taylor's book is a "Plan of a Farm House and Offices" (FIG. 4.3). Although it refers to a farmhouse, the design is of an elegant one-storey, hipped-roof cottage whose facade featuring "three flat arched recesses" reflects the influence of nineteenth-century neoclassicism.[11]

From the 1790s, with the flowering of the Romantic movement, there is a growing fascination in England with the cottage orné, which we first encountered in chapter 1.[12] Charles Middleton's 1793 architectural pattern book, *Picturesque and Architectural Views for Cottages, Farm Houses, and Country Villas*, ignores the need for cottages for "the poorer sort of country people" and concentrates on cottages "built at the entrance to or in different parts of, parks or pleasure grounds."[13] Playing on the theme of

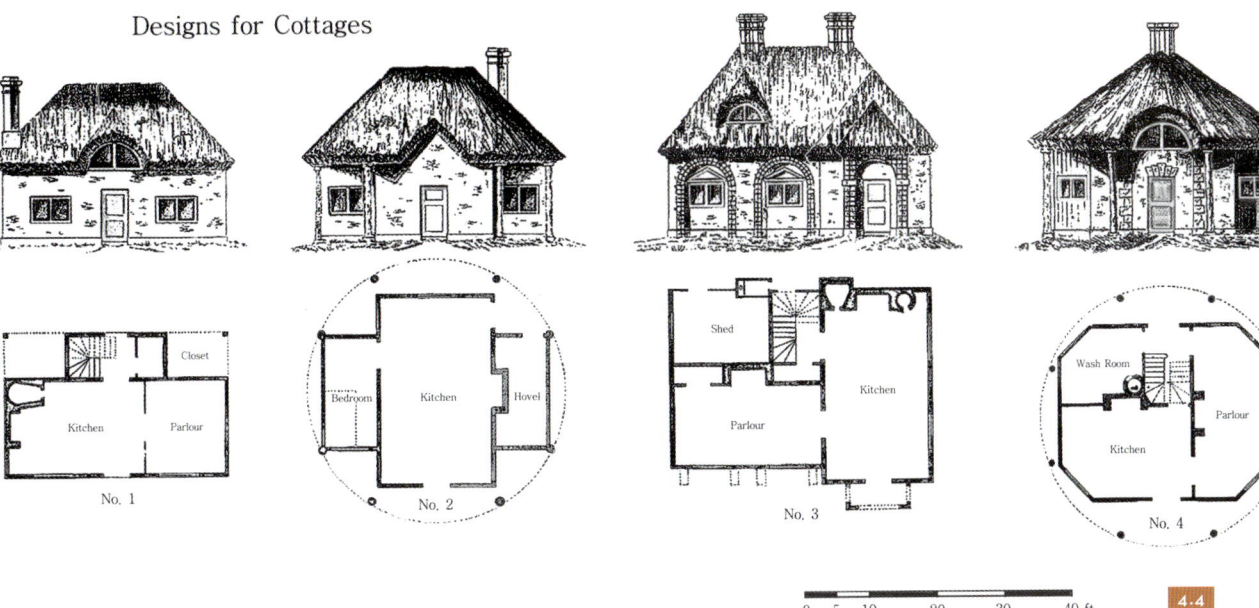

4.4 *Designs for Cottages.* Thatch roofs define all four cottages; three of the roofs are hipped, and one is conical. The roofs are higher than normal, as thatch roofs need to shed rainwater quickly. Three of the modest cottages have simple symmetrical front elevations, while the fourth cottage has a pleasing asymmetry. All four cottages are decidedly ornamental, though their small size suggests they could be affordable options for labourers. Drawn by Ho Yin Lee after Charles Middleton, *Picturesque and Architectural Views for Cottages, Farm Houses, and Country Villas* (Farnborough, UK: Gregg International, 1972); n.p.; first published 1793 (London).

rusticity, some of Middleton's designs feature thatched roofs and columns made from the "rude trunks of trees" (FIG. 4.4). Such cottages appealed to people of means who professed to prefer the simple life associated with cottage living.[14]

Other examples of the cottage orné include plate VII in John Plaw's *Sketches for Country Houses, Villas, and Rural Dwellings* (1800) (FIG. 1.4) and plate V in Edmund Bartell's *Hints for Picturesque Improvements in Ornamental Cottages, and Their Scenery* (1804) (FIG. 4.5).[15] The interest in the cottage orné in pattern books continues through the mid-nineteenth century, waning only after the 1830s; in contrast, cottages for labourers receive less attention.[16]

Turning from English and Irish architectural pattern books, which are almost

Design Sources

interchangeable, to those of Scotland, we see that there is a distinctive Scottish character—a certain robustness—to the designs presented.[17] In addition to Loudon's 1833 *Encyclopaedia*, mentioned above and examined in detail later, George Smith (1793–1877), in his *Essay on the Construction of Cottages Suited for the Dwellings of the Labouring Classes* (1834), proposes nine designs for single and "combined" (double) cottages.[18] Four of his designs are for double cottages, one of which (plate VI) has a hipped roof and is similar to Woods's "Cottages with Three Rooms" (FIG. 4.2), but here the massive walls are two feet thick and built of rubble stone.[19] In promoting the double cottage, Smith writes, "This cottage can be built cheaper than two single ones; and, in general, these double cottages are found to be warmer and fully as comfortable as single ones."[20]

From this brief scrutiny of architectural pattern book designs, we see that designs for utilitarian cottages tend to be plainer, proportions simpler (no doubt related to their smaller size), but generally pleasing, whereas those for ornamental cottages are animated with rustic elements or details from prevailing styles, and sometimes intended for picturesque grounds. In some cases, as seen in Taylor's plan for "Farm House and Offices," the simplicity of more utilitarian cottages is combined with a restrained neoclassical elegance.

MIGRATION OF COTTAGE DESIGNS TO UPPER CANADA

There is scant evidence to suggest that emigrants arrived with architectural pattern books in hand, but we do know that several Upper Canada architects had pattern books in their offices. This is hardly surprising, as

4.10 Design 1. Loudon's compact hipped-roof cottage sits securely on a raised terrace. Steps lead to an unusually designed portico: instead of leading to a single entrance door, they lead to two—one for the basement, and one for the ground floor. Nonetheless, the inspiration is Palladian, but with a decidedly Scottish feel. (The shelves pressed against the side elevation are for beehives, and there is a small dog kennel below them. Above the doorways is a dovecote with four openings.)
Drawn by Ho Yin Lee after J.C. Loudon, *An Encyclopaedia of Cottage, Farm, and Villa Architecture and Furniture [. . .]* (London: Longman, Orme, Brown, Green, and Longmans, 1839), 14. Archives and Special Collections, Western Libraries.

trunk or carpetbag, although perhaps he had access to a copy during his apprenticeship with Toronto architect William Thomas (1799–1860).[34]

Whether Smith designed the Small Gothic Cottage or not, we are left with another question: Was the design novel and influential, or did it simply "capture" an already popular houseform? The answer is a complex one.

In addition to the impact of architects, architectural pattern books, and emigrant guides—and possibly of the British military[35]—on housing designs, English, Irish, and Scottish emigrants to Upper Canada of course carried memories of the cultural landscapes they left behind, and these would have included a variety of cottages, including lodges "at the gate." Once settled in their adopted country, the newcomers would certainly have considered the hipped-roof cottage as one of the familiar and practical choices for urban, suburban, rural, and—arguably—more picturesque locations.[36]

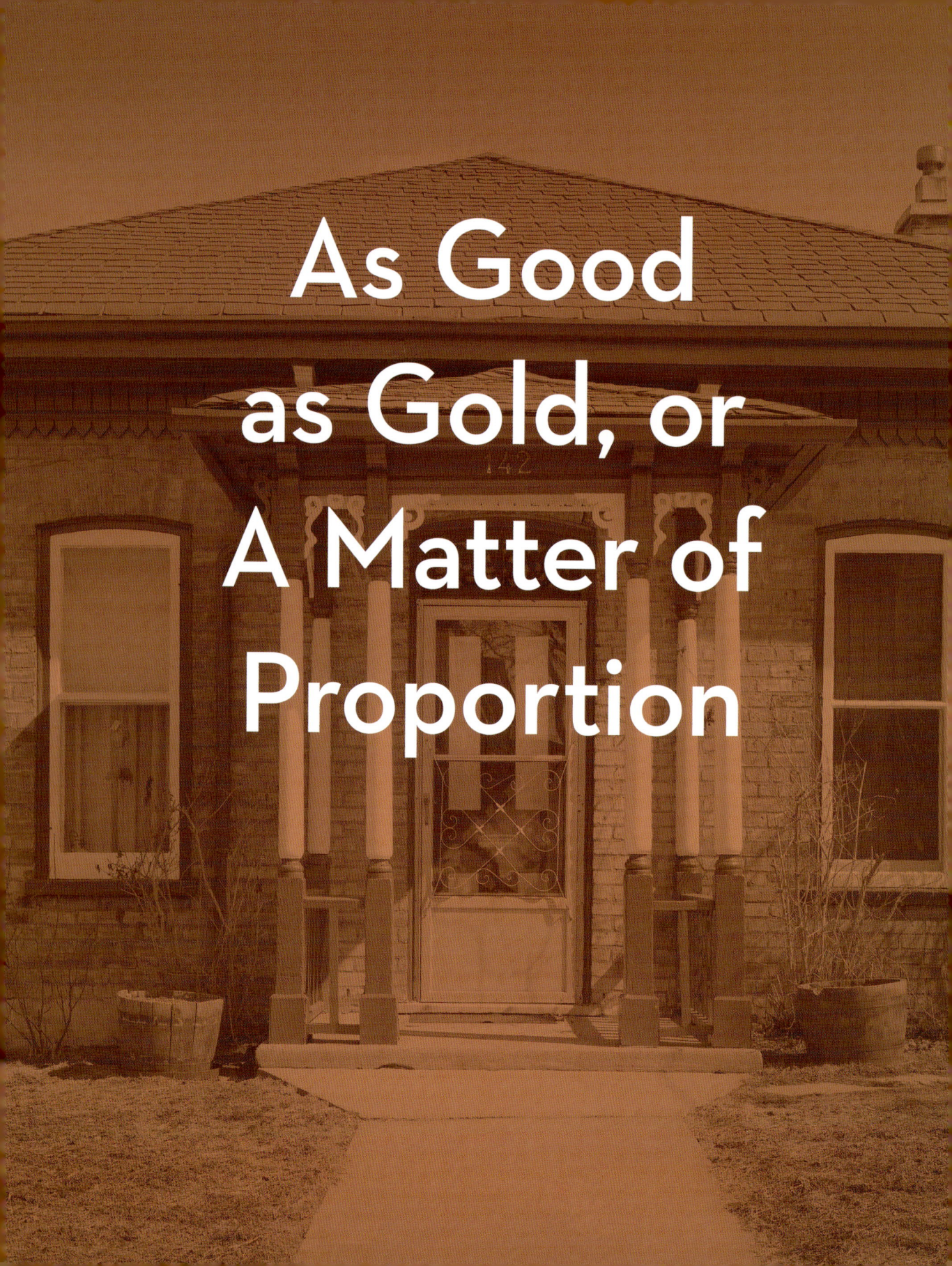

5

Each time we approach the cottage…
we catch our breath, attracted particularly
by the beautiful front doorway, which leads
into a gracious and welcoming entrance hall.
JULIA BECK, letter to Lynne DiStefano

TOGETHER WITH ITS CHARACTERISTIC symmetry and small scale, it is the good proportions of the one-storey, hipped-roof cottage that account for its immediate appeal. James Gibbs (1674–1754), an architect born in Scotland and trained in Rome, expressed the importance of good proportion this way:

> For it is not the Bulk of a Fabrick, the Richness and Quantity of the Materials, the Multiplicity of Lines, nor the Gaudiness of the Finishing, that give the Grace or Beauty and Grandeur to a Building; but the *Proportion of the Parts to one another and to the Whole,* whether entirely plain, or enriched with a few Ornaments properly disposed [*italics added*].[1]

To achieve "Justness of Proportion,"[2] Vitruvius and later Palladio relied on modules or units to determine the relationship of building parts. For example, a basic unit taken from one of the dimensions of a classical order (a column and its associated entablature) would be used to determine the dimensions of other parts of the order and the spaces between columns.[3] Various multiples of the basic unit determined each building part and the

Constructing the Ontario Cottage

6.1

The rough board-and-batten surface, with its pronounced verticality, appealed to followers of Andrew Jackson Downing (1815–1852), the mid-nineteenth-century American architect known for his promotion of Gothic Revival. Tongue-and-groove siding, on the other hand, was likely chosen for its flat surface and water tightness.

Brick, whether burnt or unburnt, was an early and widespread building material, used for foundations, walls, and chimneys. The Wilderness (c. 1816–17) in Niagara-on-the-Lake is stucco over brick (PLATE 6.8),[2] while Woodburn (1834) in Beamsville has exposed brickwork (PLATE 6.9). Close to a decade later, *The British American Cultivator* could report,

> Letter from James McGregor, Clangrigor Castle, Con 11, Lot 6, Howard Township [probably in Ridgetown], saying he had built a house 31′ × 21′ of unburnt brick last summer. He agrees ... that it is superior to [timber-]frame. His house is built

6

By the mid-nineteenth century Ontario contained more than 145,000 dwellings, the majority of which were built of logs. Of the total, approximately 12 per cent were shanties; 40 per cent were made of round logs and 5 per cent of hewn logs; 37 per cent were frame houses; and brick and stone each accounted for approximately 3 per cent.
BRIAN COFFEY, "Factors Affecting the Use of Construction Materials in Early Ontario"

EARLY HIPPED-ROOF COTTAGES in Ontario, such as that illustrated in H.F. Ainslie's *Settler's House on the Thames* 1842 (FIG. 6.1), are frequently of log or timber-frame construction, though mud/clay construction, as seen in The Mud Cottage (c. 1830) in Sparta (PLATE 6.1), is also found. Clapboard siding, a form of horizontal sheathing for timber-frame or balloon-frame construction, as seen in Rowan House (c. 1843) in Demorestville (PLATE 6.2) and the Alwington Avenue cottage (1854–55) in Kingston (PLATES 6.3 + 6.4), is found throughout the nineteenth century.

Less popular are two other forms of sheathing: board-and-batten and tongue and groove.[1] One of the few examples of a board-and-batten hipped-roof cottage is found in the St. David Street cottage (c. 1870) in Mitchell, northwest of Stratford (PLATE 6.5); and, in Goderich on Wellington Street South (c. 1850), there is a handsome tongue-and-groove–sided cottage where the siding is scored to imitate ashlar construction (PLATES 6.6 + 6.7).

6.1 H.F. Ainslie (1803–1879), *Settler's House on the Thames*, 1842, watercolour and pen-and-ink on wove paper, support: 10 1/5 × 14 inches. This small hipped-roof cottage with inset chimneys, most likely of log or timber-frame construction, sits on newly cleared land above the Thames River. The building appears to rest on regularly placed log sections. Library and Archives Canada.

cottage-fashion with a pavilion [hipped] roof; the chimney is in the centre of the house with doors and windows opposite each other.[3]

Although brick cottages are found throughout the province, especially in the numerous areas with clay deposits, there are notable concentrations in such places as Brantford, London, Port Hope, Stratford, and Toronto. The popularity of brick construction in London, for example, can be seen in building progress reports in the *London Free Press*.[4]

Until the late nineteenth century, the composition of local clays and kiln conditions were key factors in determining the colour of brickwork. Buff (or yellow) brick and occasionally light red brick with an orange cast feature prominently in Brantford, as seen in the Albion Street cottages (PLATE 3.7; 1872 on the left, 1874 on the right); in London, Templar Cottage (c. 1874) (PLATE 6.10) and Nathaniel Reid Cottage (c. 1878) (PLATE 6.11); and in Stratford, an 1870 cottage on James Street (PLATE 6.12). Meanwhile, red brick makes an appearance by the 1850s in Port Hope, as seen in The Belvedere (PLATE 6.13). By the 1890s, manufactured brick in a variety of colours is readily accessible from main centres of production such as Milton and Toronto, leading to more consistent quality but a loss of regional distinctiveness.

Limestone, also an early building material for foundations, chimneys, and walls, is primarily found in two extensive areas: Eastern Ontario, including north to Ottawa along the Rideau Canal, and along the Niagara Escarpment in Southwestern Ontario. A Scottish mason in Upper Canada described, in 1820, the availability of stone in a letter to a friend in Glasgow:

> There is [*sic*] plenty of stones in various parts of Canada: about Kingston, it is all rock together, and at many other places up the lake. There is an acquaintance of mine who has a lot about thirty miles from York [Toronto], where he says there is plenty of free-stone: but there are other parts of the country where there is no stone; such as Colonel Talbot's settlement, and upon the river Thames.[5]

In tracing Scottish architecture in Ontario, Anson Bailey Cutts remarks,

> Log cabins were superseded by one-story cut-stone cottages in the towns, for liberal inducements in the way of free lots were offered those who built of stone... The design... was as simple as their four-square plan: a central hallway flanked by rooms two deep, producing a symmetrical facade in the centre of which was the front door with single windows to either side. Porches or even stoops were conspicuously absent, and exterior ornamentation was confined to chaste Georgian cornices and, in exceptional instances, finely carved stone mouldings around doors and windows. Roofs were either hipped or gabled at the ends.[6]

Whether built by Scots or other emigrant groups, examples of limestone hipped-roof cottages in Ontario include a rural cottage, Clapp–Palmer House (c. 1841) near Consecon (PLATES 6.14 + 6.15), and, farther to the east, Charles Place (c. 1830) in Kingston (PLATES 2.2 + 2.3). Examples in the southwest of the province include Perry–Scroggie House (c. 1862) in Guelph (PLATE 5.3) and Wood–Simpson House (c. 1856) near St. Marys (PLATE 6.16). Far removed from the Niagara Escarpment, St. Marys, nicknamed the "Stonetown," is an anomaly within the physiography of Southern Ontario.

Besides limestone and the occasional use of fieldstone and cut granite, as in McDougall Cottage (c. 1858) in Cambridge (PLATES 9.3 + 9.4), the use of cobblestones offers a striking if rare variation of stone construction. In this method, brought to Ontario from Upstate New York in the 1830s, small conical-shaped stones are laid in mortar in even courses. In what is technically a veneer, only the ends of the cobblestones, which may be embedded by as much as six inches, project from the surface of the wall.[7] Paris boasts the majority of cobblestone buildings in Ontario, including a number of Ontario Cottages, such as the Queen Street cottage (c. 1852) (PLATES 6.17 + 6.18) and Hamilton Place (1839–44) (PLATE 6.20).

Stucco, made of lime, sand, and water, was sometimes applied as a smooth finish coat for buildings. For example, Colborne Lodge (1837) in Toronto (PLATE 6.19) and Hooey Cottage (c. 1855) in Port Hope (PLATE 5.2) were stuccoed. Stucco as a surface treatment remained popular throughout the century.

Whether brick, stone, or wood was used in building cottages, availability is only part of the story. As building-construction historian Brian Coffey explains, skilled labour was necessary for construction in the mid-nineteenth century, especially for houses of brick or stone. This in turn required a certain amount of capital, as seen in the substantial houses built by prosperous farmers, innkeepers, merchants, and urban professionals. Another factor was the preference for specific materials by certain groups—for instance, stone by the Scots.[8]

Later, into the twentieth century, concrete, including rock-faced hollow concrete block, was occasionally used for cottage construction. In the early 1900s, Larkin Farms, an extensive mixed farm in Niagara-on-the-Lake, built a series of concrete cottages for its workers (PLATE 6.21), an initiative that reminds us of efforts in the late eighteenth century to improve the working conditions of labourers. To the credit of Larkin Farms and its architect, an owner—decades later—could describe his cottage as "the most efficiently designed house I've ever lived in."[9]

PLATE 6.1
The Mud Cottage

Sparta Line, Sparta,
c. 1830 or earlier

PLATE 6.2
Rowan House
Demorestville, c. 1843

PLATE 6.3
Alwington Avenue, Kingston, 1854–55

PLATE 6.4
Alwington Avenue, Kingston, 1854–55: detail

PLATE 6.5
St. David Street,
Mitchell, c. 1870

PLATE 6.6
Wellington Street South, Goderich, c. 1850

PLATE 6.7
Wellington Street South, Goderich, c. 1850: detail

PLATE 6.8
The Wilderness

King Street,
Niagara-on-the-Lake, 1816–17

PLATE 6.9
Woodburn

King Street,
Beamsville, 1834

PLATE 6.10
Templar Cottage

Talbot Street,
London, c. 1874

PLATE 6.11
Nathaniel Reid Cottage

Waterloo Street,
London, c. 1878

PLATE 6.12

James Street,
Stratford, 1870

PLATE 6.13
The Belvedere

Augusta Street,
Port Hope, c. 1850

PLATE 6.14
Clapp-Palmer House
near Consecon, c. 1841

PLATE 6.15
Clapp-Palmer House
near Consecon, c. 1841: detail

PLATE 6.16
Wood–Simpson House

near St. Marys, c. 1856

PLATE 6.17
Queen Street,
Paris, c. 1852

PLATE 6.18
Queen Street,
Paris, c. 1852

PLATE 6.19
Colborne Lodge

Colborne Lodge Drive,
Toronto, 1837

PLATE 6.20
Hamilton Place

Grand River Street North, Paris, 1839–44

PLATE 6.21

Niagara River Parkway, Niagara-on-the-Lake, early 1900s

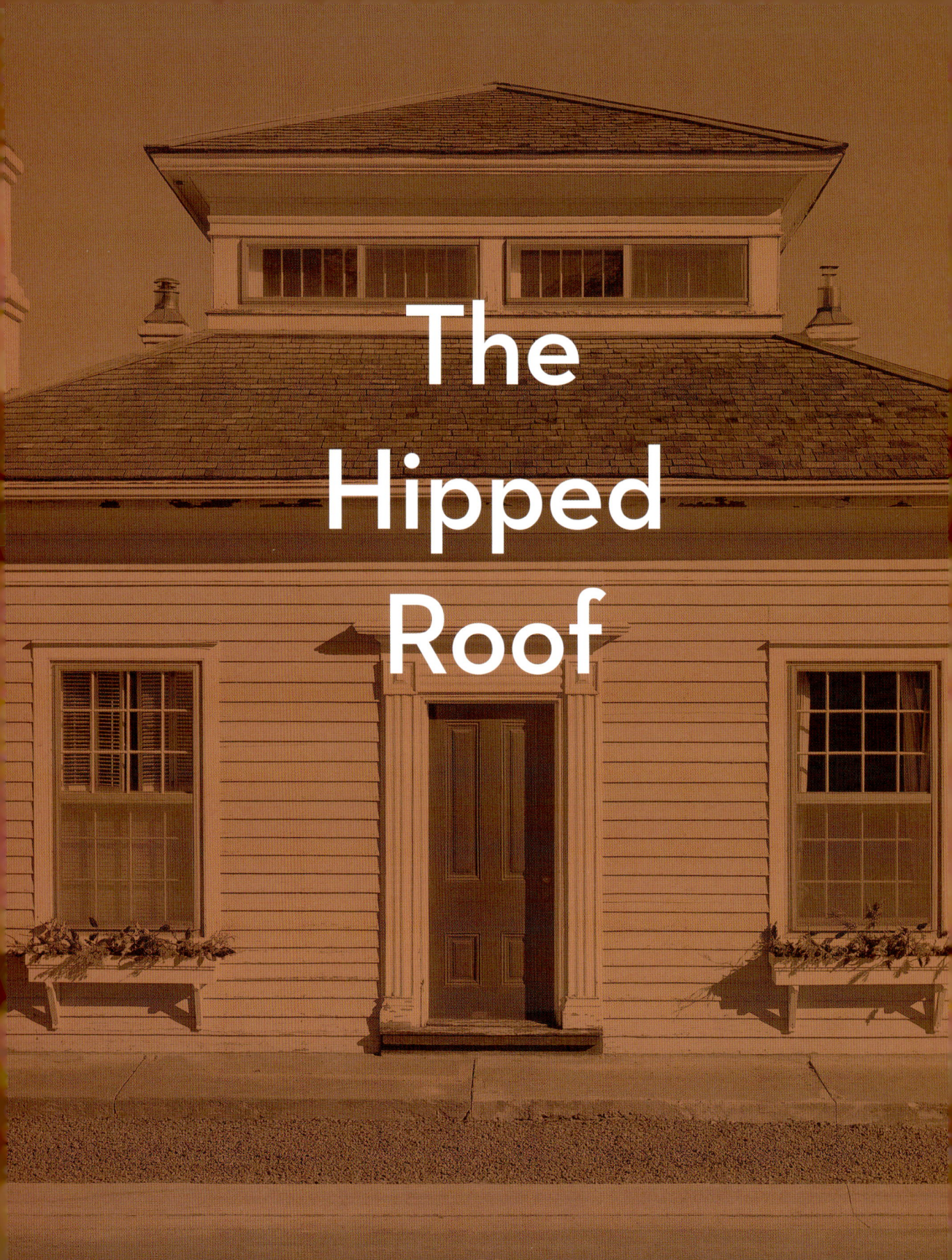

The Hipped Roof

7

> There was a most ingenious Architect who had contrived a new Method for building Houses, by beginning at the Roof, and working downwards to the Foundation; which he justified to me by the like Practice of those two prudent Insects the Bee and the Spider.
> JONATHAN SWIFT, *Gulliver's Travels*, 1726

GRAVITY, AMONG OTHER THINGS, works against the fanciful approach to house construction conveyed in the epigraph that opens this chapter. But the critical role of the roof as an enclosing feature of buildings is clear. For the Ontario Cottage, the *kind* of roof—its hipped or four-sided roof—is also *the* defining element. It sets this type of cottage apart from other types, especially those with gable roofs.

What makes a hipped roof? It is a roof distinguished by its roof planes (or sides), usually four, sloping down from a ridge to each of four eaves, forming a truncated pyramid (**FIG. 7.1**). Some Ontario Cottages feature a pyramidal roof, a hipped roof with no ridge and all four planes meeting at a point. (See **FIG. 7.2** for isometric drawings of various hipped roofs.) The appeal of this kind of roof may be in its ability to give a "centralizing aspect" to a building, with all the roof planes leading up to a shared central point or ridge.[1] The hipped roof also conveys an enhanced sense of protection: Vitruvius equated the roof form to the hard shell of a tortoise.[2] The feeling of protection is sometimes enhanced by noticeably deep or wide eaves (the overhang of a roof beyond its walls), as seen in the King Street West cottage (1840) in Colborne (**PLATE 7.1**).

7.1 John Powell Hunt (1842–1932), *Maple Cottage*, c. 1883, watercolour on paper, 7 × 11½ inches. Museum London.

The framing of the hipped roof is straightforward. In technical terms, the outline of the roof is formed by a ridge beam (the uppermost horizontal edge of the roof), hip rafters (along the edges of the sloping roof planes), and eaves boards (the edges of the lowest horizontal rectangular plane). Common rafters (that run from the ridge beam to the eaves boards) and jack rafters (that run from the hip rafters to the eaves boards) are secured to a wall plate and support the roofing materials. To complete the roof structure, the bottom ends of each pair of inverted-V roof rafters are tied with a horizontal ceiling joist, thus creating a simple rigid triangular form that acts as a truss. (See FIG. 7.3 for an isometric drawing showing hipped-roof construction.)

To bring light into the otherwise dark attic, there are sometimes windows. These range from a perky small window centred in a gable over the front door, as in the Small Gothic Cottage, to a belvedere that seems to add another storey to the cottage, as in the Marysville Road cottage (c. 1840) in Lonsdale (PLATES 7.2 + 7.3), Van Norman–Guiler Cottage (c. 1842) in Normandale (PLATES 5.4 + 5.5), and Clapp–Palmer House (c. 1841) near Consecon (PLATES 6.14 + 6.15). (In the latter case, the additional weight is usually distributed downward through corner posts that rest on ceiling joists.)

In the nineteenth century, the structural framework, once complete, was covered with wooden shingles, slates, or metal sheets, which are fixed to horizontally laid battens attached to the rafters. Some of these early roofing materials survive, but many cottages are re-roofed with twentieth-century materials, such as asphalt shingles or standing seam metal panels.

Compare the hipped-roof cottage to the small gable-roof house, a type of cottage also prevalent in Ontario (FIG. 7.4). As the name

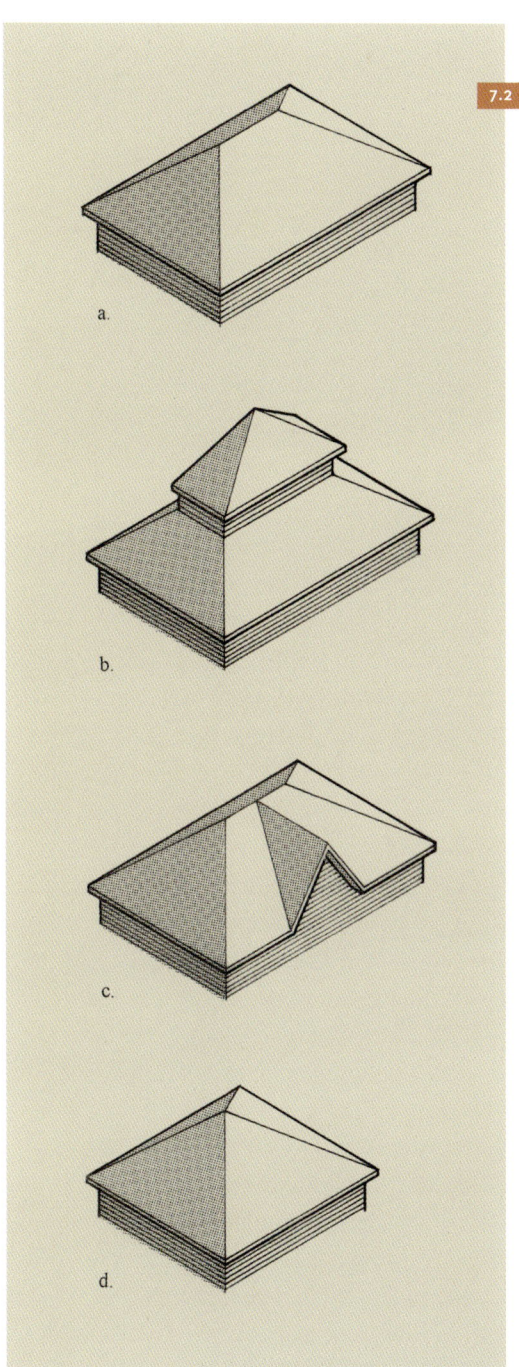

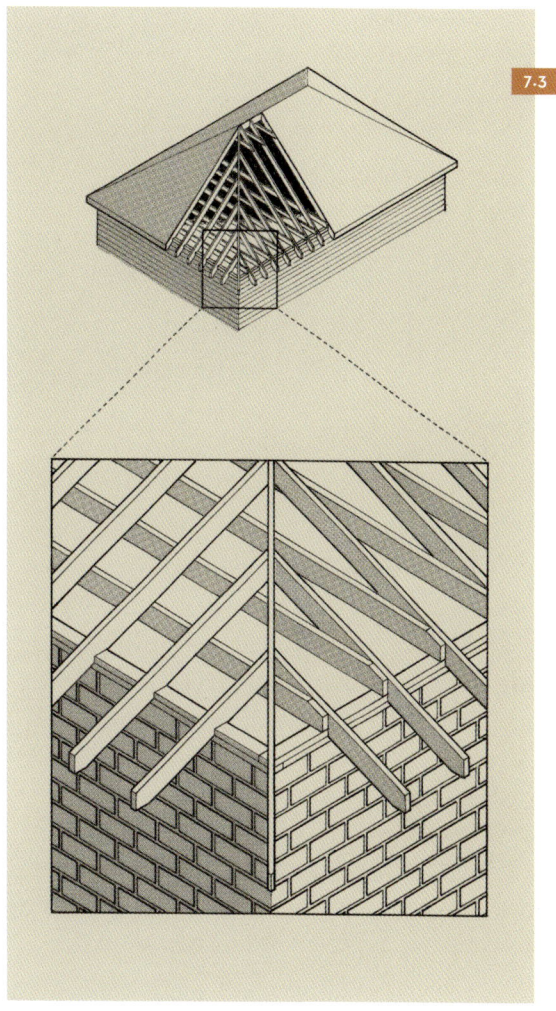

7.2 Isometric drawings of types of hipped roofs: (a) hipped roof; (b) hipped roof with belvedere; (c) hipped roof with gable; and (d) hipped roof on a projection. Drawn by Ho Yin Lee.

7.3 Isometric drawing of hipped-roof construction. Drawn by Ho Yin Lee.

7.4 Philip John Bainbrigge (1817–1881), *Lower Bytown*, 1841, watercolour on wove paper, 9½ × 6½ inches. The gable-roofed cottage with a veranda was the home of Lieutenant-Colonel John By, the English engineer responsible for the construction of the Rideau Canal. Library and Archives Canada.

implies, a gable roof is contained within two gable-end walls, with two roof planes sloping down from a ridge to eaves on opposite sides of the building. (The hipped roof, in contrast, sits on walls of equal height, which makes the roof easier to construct.) The gable roof presents no economic advantage over the hipped roof, as it uses the same quantity of wood to build,[3] but it does offer the practical benefit of additional headroom in the spaces that abut the gable-end sides. A drawback of the gable roof, however, is its lesser resistance to wind pressure than the hipped roof, making it less stable in extreme wind conditions.[4]

As with gable roofs, hipped roofs show considerable variation in pitch. Pitch is the angle or steepness of the planes of a roof; decisions about pitch are influenced by several factors, especially climate. In milder climates, where rain is the main consideration, a pitch range between 30 and 45 degrees is adequate for throwing off rainwater.[5] In colder climates, a steeper pitch ranging from 45 to as much as 60 degrees helps prevent excessive snow build-up that could overburden the roof structure, leading to collapse. Regarding an appropriate roof angle for a northern climate, the author of one early-nineteenth-century Scottish pattern book recommends (without further explanation) the square pitch, "where the roof height equals one half the width of a house," basically a 45-degree roof pitch.[6]

Another consideration in choosing a roof pitch is cost. A steeper roof is more costly to construct, as it requires more materials—and since it weighs more, it requires heavier supporting walls and a stronger foundation, further adding to the structure's cost. Although the hipped roof of the Ontario Cottage, generally a low-slung, more modest building, usually has a relatively shallow pitch, elevation studies of representative cottages show a range of roof pitches (FIGS. 5.1–5.5).

In the next chapter, we look at another distinguishing and obvious feature of many Ontario Cottages: their verandas.

PLATE 7.1

King Street West,
Colborne, c. 1840

The Hipped Roof

PLATE 7.2
Marysville Road,
Lonsdale, c. 1840

PLATE 7.3
Marysville Road, Lonsdale, c. 1840

The Veranda

8

Nine steep steps led from the driveway up to the front verandah. The elevation gave it the dignity of a stage and everything that happened there took on the aura and significance of performance.
ARUNDHATI ROY, *The God of Small Things*

ALTHOUGH NOT AS ESSENTIAL to the Ontario Cottage as its hipped roof, the veranda is a typical and striking component of many cottage designs. The description of a twentieth-century Indian veranda in Arundhati Roy's *The God of Small Things* could easily apply to a nineteenth-century veranda in Ontario. This is not surprising; the earliest local verandas were most likely influenced by the integrated veranda of the Anglo-Indian bungalow.[1] Although such covered porches are found in a variety of Ontario houses,[2] their use for one-storey, hipped-roof cottages is closest to their Indian (now Bangladeshi) source.

ORIGINS
We encountered the bungalow as a distinct houseform in the first chapter of this book. Like the form itself, the term "bungalow" originated in India. The name is from the Hindi word *Bangla*, which means "of or belonging to Bengal."[3] As Anthony D. King writes in *The Bungalow: The Production of a Global Culture*, the primary features of the indigenous Bengal hut are "its free-standing and single-storey structure, the plinth, the pitched, thatched

roof and the verandah" (FIG. 8.1).⁴ By the end of the eighteenth century, what came to be called the Anglo-Indian bungalow, a modification of the Bengal hut, was well developed.⁵ Distinguished by its size and number of rooms, including rooms covered by the veranda roof, it became one of the houseforms used by Europeans in India during the late eighteenth century and throughout much of the nineteenth.⁶ The veranda is integrated: it is an extension of the main roof of the house—the roof is drawn out, extending over a plinth, creating a sheltered outdoor space.

The word "veranda" is also found in the Portuguese and Spanish languages, the Spanish word *varanda* in fact predating the Anglicized equivalent, "veranda" (also spelled "verandah").⁷ But the veranda as an architectural element can be traced even further back. As English architect John Buonarotti Papworth (1775–1847) points out in his 1818 book *Rural Residences*, "the verandah is of Eastern and of very ancient origin."⁸

GLOBAL APPEAL

The spread of the bungalow with an integrated veranda beyond colonial India was hastened by British publications about India, the building work of the Royal Engineers, and numerous architectural pattern books that included designs based on the Indian bungalow.⁹ As mentioned in chapter 1, in *Sketches for Country Houses, Villas, and Rural Dwellings* (1800), John Plaw, an English-Canadian architect, helped popularize the veranda with his design for a dwelling "with a Viranda in the manner of an Indian Bungalow" (FIG. 1.4).¹⁰

8.1 George Chinnery (1774–1852), *Thatched Indian Hut with a Woman and Child and a Tethered Cow at the Entrance*, n.d., pen-and-ink on paper, 7 × 9 inches. This Bengal hut, with its curved ridge and four sides, is known as the *chauchala* type, as opposed to the *dochala* type, which has a curved ridge and two sides with gable ends. In this drawing, the front section of the hut's roof extends over a well-used outdoor space, the veranda. See Anthony D. King, *The Bungalow: The Production of a Global Culture* (New York: Oxford University Press, 1995), 22. The Morgan Library & Museum.

By the 1830s, the veranda was so common in Ontario that Catharine Parr Traill could report in *The Backwoods of Canada* (1836) that "few houses, either log or frame, are without them."[11]

The ongoing appeal of the veranda relates primarily to its practicality. In tropical and subtropical climates, it helps insulate the interior of the house from the full impact of the sun. In cold climates, such as Ontario's, a veranda offers the same advantage during the late spring, summer, and early fall when the sun is high. In the late fall, winter, and early spring when the sun is lower, and depending upon its orientation, it serves as a passive heat reservoir, helping conserve the warmth of the sun "trapped" in the building's exterior walls. In the verandas of many Ontario houses, climbing vines, winding themselves around veranda supports, provide additional sun-shading during the warmer months but limited solar-heat trapping during the cooler ones.[12] The veranda also protects from rain and snow.

Although the veranda served a practical purpose, in the nineteenth century its aesthetic qualities drew a mixed response.

Papworth writes in *Rural Residences* that "no decorations have so successfully varied the dull sameness of modern structures in the metropolis, as the *verandah*, the *lengthened window*, and the *balcony*; they have produced an intrinsic elegance [*italics in the original*]."[13] Praise of the veranda is echoed by Traill, who opines in *The Backwoods of Canada* that "these stoups [verandas] are really a considerable ornament."[14] Another Ontario writer, Emerald D. Fowler, expresses an opposing view in an article for the June 1882 edition of *Rose-Belford's Canadian Monthly and National Review*:

> If a house has any architectural pretension whatever, a veranda never harmonizes with it; it cannot; it is a mery [very] flimsy excrescence, or an incongruous addition stuck on. Shade must be had in the great heat of summer, you say. Admitted. But there are many kinds of blinds which answer the purpose well enough, and, what is more, accommodate themselves to the time of day. Best of all, however, are shade trees.[15]

8.2 Prospect Cottage, also known as Mallory Cottage, between Cobourg and Grafton (lot 33, concession A, Haldimand), early nineteenth century. Supported by treillages, the veranda with its integrated roof runs around three sides of the building. A belvedere sits at the apex of the hipped roof and lights four bedrooms and a hall on the second floor. From *Illustrated Historical Atlas of the Counties of Northumberland and Durham, Ont.* (Toronto: H. Belden, 1878), 83. Archives and Special Collections, Western Libraries.

Fowler may be correct that shade trees might be best for shade, but his dismissive comments about the veranda are harder to defend. As we have seen, not all verandas are "stuck on" or "tacked on."[16] In some of the earliest examples of the veranda in Ontario, the veranda roof is integrated, extending the main roof of the house. An example of this kind of roof is seen in Prospect Cottage (early 1800s) between Cobourg and Grafton, a well-proportioned red brick building with a veranda along three sides. Here, there is a seamless transition between the main roof of the cottage and the roof of the veranda (FIG. 8.2). Another example is Creek Cottage (1840s) in Ayr (PLATE 8.1).

While verandas with integrated roofs are more directly linked to the traditional Bengal hut, the "tacked on" or articulated veranda, as seen in Waltham Cottage (c. 1856; veranda later) in Bowmanville (PLATE 8.2) and the Byng Avenue cottage (1832) in Cambridge (PLATE 8.3), had both structural and functional advantages. The veranda roof simplified the

134   THE ONTARIO COTTAGE

8.3 Anonymous, Drumsnab, photograph of original drawing, c. 1834. As described by Sir James Edward Alexander in *L'Acadie* (London: Henry Colburn, 1849), 230, the cottage occupies "the most picturesque spot near Toronto.... The mansion is roomy, and of one story, with a broad verandah. It is seated among fields and woods, at the edge of a slope; at the bottom winds a river, opposite is a most singular conical hill, like an immense...tumulus for the dead." The cottage's integrated veranda and high-pitched hipped-roof are reminiscent of the Anglo-Indian bungalow. Special Collections, Toronto Reference Library.

construction of the main roof and at the same time allowed a different—and presumably more functional—pitch for its roof. It also offered the opportunity to modulate the shape of the roof. Rather than a straight roof pitch, the roof could be curved (or bellcast), much like the gentle shape of an awning.[17]

During the early nineteenth century, both types of veranda roof were common features for cottages in Ontario. For example, both appear in the drawings of John George Howard, the prominent nineteenth-century Toronto-based architect. One of his few dated cottage drawings (1834) shows an ample hipped-roof structure with an articulated veranda roof on three sides. There are also two drawings for cottages with integrated verandas. The first is for Howard's own cottage in Toronto, an unusual, partially polygonal form with a veranda along the polygonal part of the cottage; this design was realized in 1837 as Colborne Lodge, in what is now High Park (PLATE 6.19). The second is an octagonal cottage with a veranda on five contiguous sides, a variation of the Colborne Lodge design.[18]

Drumsnab (c. 1834; second storey added 1850) on Castle Frank Drive in Toronto (FIG. 8.3) also boasts a veranda with an integrated roof, while the veranda of the Bank Street North cottage (c. 1837) in Millbrook is an early example of the articulated kind (PLATES 8.4 + 8.5).[19] Other examples of verandas with articulated roofs include Rokewood (1847) in Woodstock (PLATE 2.5), and the Main Street cottage (1855) in Odessa (PLATES 8.6 + 8.7). For probable ease of construction and perhaps reasons of economy, the articulated veranda roof became the norm.

The Veranda

135

8.4 Roselands (demolished), Seaton Street, Toronto, c. 1815, coloured stereoscopic photograph, 1860. Trellis work, mounted on the veranda supports, forms arches for each bay. In the first bay on the left are (from left to right) Mrs. James Unwin, Sarah Unwin, and Polly Parsons (standing). Charles Unwin and Elizabeth Unwin pose in front of the veranda. The Unwins were later occupants of Roselands, which was built and first occupied by Samuel Ridout, who worked as a clerk in the Surveyor General's Office. Special Collections, Toronto Reference Library.

A "SORT OF OUTER ROOM"

Along with aesthetics and the more practical benefits of heating and cooling a house, a big part of the veranda's appeal was its role as an outdoor room—a "sort of outer room," as Traill referred to it.[20] A.J. Downing, the influential nineteenth-century American architect, summarized the social functions of the veranda as "the resting place, lounging spot, and place of social resort of the whole family."[21]

He probably should have added "weather depending"; nonetheless, it is clear from nineteenth-century texts and photographs that verandas were enjoyed extensively. In 1832, Ontario resident Thomas William Magrath described how his family used their veranda:

> We pass our leisure hours in it during the fine weather, choosing the shady, and sheltered side, according to the sun, or wind; and frequently sitting there with candles until bed time; with the occasional annoyance, however, of the troublesome moskitoes; but where can we expect to find perfect enjoyment?[22]

A mid-nineteenth-century stereoscopic photograph captures the Unwin family posing within—and in front of—their shaded veranda (FIG. 8.4).

8.5 The Knight family posing on the veranda of Drew Cottage, Rathbourne Avenue, Woodstock, c. 1895. Drew Cottage was built in 1833, a decade in which generous Regency Cottages were built frequently with deep verandas that ran around three sides of the building. (See PLATE 2.4 for a contemporary photo of the cottage.) Archives of Ontario.

A photograph from much later in the century reveals how the veranda straddles the boundary between private and public (FIG. 8.5). Here we see thirteen members of the Knight family gathered together for a group photograph at Drew Cottage in Woodstock. In this meticulously staged scene, family members are positioned in front of the cottage, some on the deck of the veranda, one in a chair on the veranda, and another in the veranda hammock. Other family members stand or sit on the grass in front. A bicycle rests against the left-hand side of the three-sided veranda, and badminton rackets are artfully held by at least two people. Nestled between the owner (fourth person from the left) and his wife is a small dark dog. Dense vines climb three of the veranda treillages and, stretching along the eaves, reach several more. A plant rests in a rustic stand near the corner of the house. Here the veranda has become a stage for showcasing the proud residents and their activities.

Of course, not all Ontario Cottages have verandas. Porches, including enclosed porches, sometimes referred to as "storm porches," were another option; examples include Lovers Lane cottage (c. 1852) in Bowmanville (PLATES 8.8 + 8.9), the Glasgow Street North cottage (c. 1877) in Guelph (PLATES 8.10 + 8.11), the Broadway Street East cottage (1845) in Paris (PLATES 8.12 + 8.13), and the Caledonia Street cottage (c. 1880) in Stratford (PLATE 8.14). More modest cottages, such as the Church Street cottage (c. 1855) in Kitchener (PLATE 5.1), are sometimes embellished by handsome entrance porches with turned wooden posts supporting a roof.

PLATE 8.1

Creek Cottage

Water Street,
Ayr, 1840s

PLATE 8.2

Waltham Cottage

Division Street,
Bowmanville, c. 1856

PLATE 8.3
Byng Avenue, Cambridge, 1832

PLATE 8.4
Bank Street North, Millbrook, c. 1837

PLATE 8.5
Bank Street North, Millbrook, c. 1837: detail

PLATE 8.6
Main Street, Odessa, 1855

PLATE 8.7
Main Street, Odessa, 1855: detail

The Veranda

PLATE 8.8
Lovers Lane,
Bowmanville, c. 1852

PLATE 8.9
Lovers Lane,
Bowmanville, c. 1852: detail

PLATE 8.10
Glasgow Street North, Guelph, c. 1877

PLATE 8.11
Glasgow Street North, Guelph, c. 1877: detail

PLATE 8.12
Broadway Street East, Paris, 1845

PLATE 8.13
Broadway Street East, Paris, 1845: detail

PLATE 8.14
Caledonia Street,
Stratford, c. 1880

Inside

9

> To be sold a brick cottage of modern style of architecture with large windows and ceilings lofty, substantially built, being intended for the permanent residence of a private gentleman—contains two parlours and three bedrooms on the ground floor, with an underground kitchen, servant's room, pantry and cellar—an outer kitchen, stable and cow shed.
>
> ADVERTISEMENT, *The Middlesex Prototype*, 1854

As we've seen, Ontario cottages have either a squarish or a more rectangular form. Three-bay cottages tend to be truncated rectangular blocks, whereas five-bay cottages are more clearly rectilinear. The building is generally oriented with one of its longer sides facing the street or road. Most cottages have a centrally placed front door, which opens directly onto a hall that runs from the front to the back (or back extension) of the house, with rooms opening off either side of the hall. An exception to this centre-hall plan is the side-hall plan found in some small three-bay cottages, where the front door is pushed to one of the side or end bays.

The typical three- or five-bay, hipped-roof cottage plan allows for many variations. An advertisement for one mid-nineteenth-century cottage property (see the epigraph that opens this chapter) hints at a plan. We can assume that it is a centre-hall plan given the number of rooms on the ground floor. By the 1830s, floor plans by John George Howard, a Toronto architect trained in England,

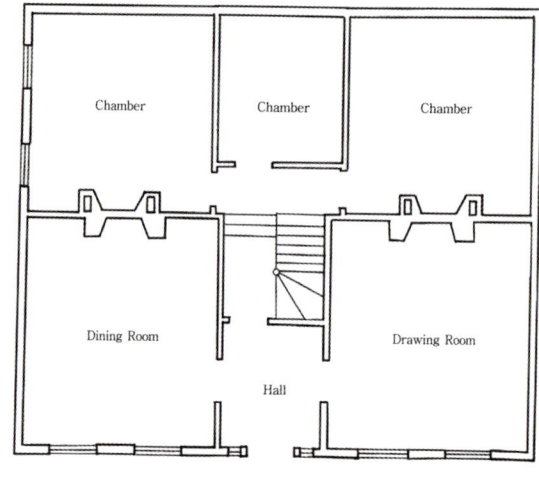

Ground Floor Plan

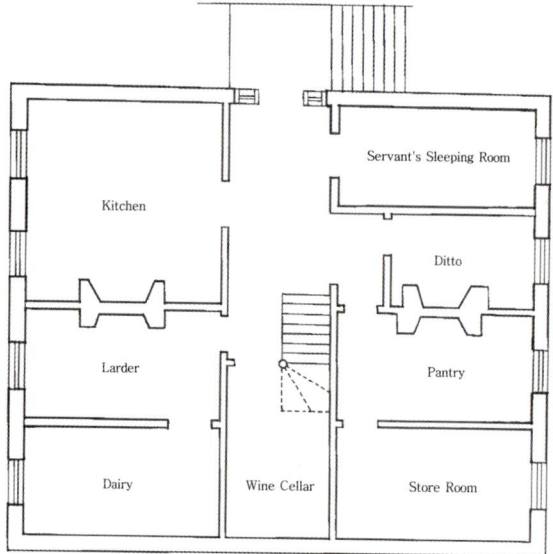

Basement Plan

illustrate possible variations on the centre-hall plan for cottages. Some of these show centre halls terminating in cross halls toward the back; others show halls leading directly to rooms at the back of the main block or to a kitchen ell attached to the main block. Yet others show the front hall terminating in a staircase that leads to either a lower or upper floor.

In the layout for an elegant cottage for H.R. Place in West Oxford (probably never constructed), Howard has included a two-part centre hall **(FIG. 9.1)**. The part closest to the front door gives admission to the more formal rooms of the cottage, with the dining room on the left and the drawing room on the right. To get to the chambers (bedrooms), one leaves the main hall, passing through an inner hall that gives access to the basement, before reaching a short cross hall with doors to three bedrooms. The basement too has a centre hall, with a wine cellar at one end and an exterior door at the other. On one side are arranged a kitchen, larder, and dairy; on the other, two sleeping rooms for servants, a pantry, and a store room.[1]

9.1 Elevation and floor plans for a cottage for H.R. Place in West Oxford. Drawn by Ho Yin Lee after John George Howard, 37–39, The Howard Collection, Special Collections, Toronto Reference Library.

9.2 Plan for the Small Gothic Cottage. Drawn by Ho Yin Lee after "A Small Gothic Cottage," *Canada Farmer* 1, no. 2 (February 1, 1864): 21.

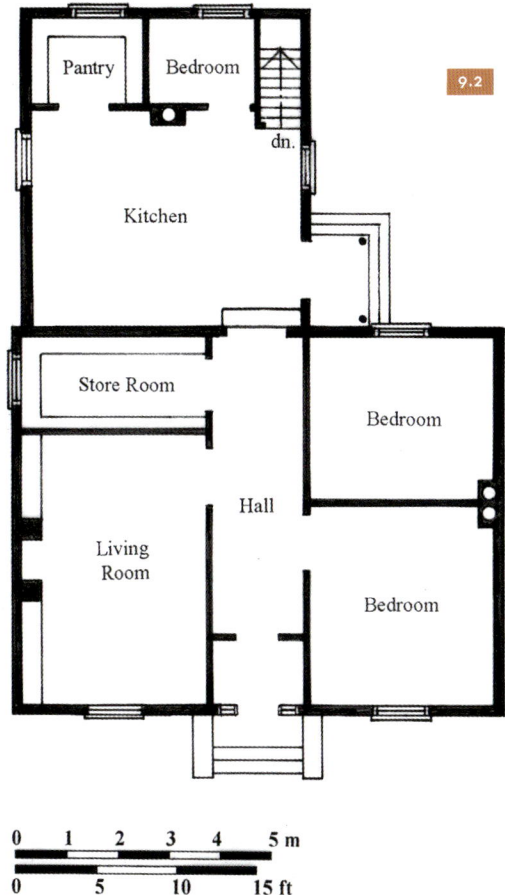

In contrast to Howard's plan for the Place cottage, that of the Small Gothic Cottage in *The Canada Farmer* issue of February 1, 1864 **(FIG. 9.2)** touts a modest centre-hall plan. The front entrance leads directly into the vestibule (a perfect airlock, in today's terms), which opens onto the main hall. On one side of the hall is an ample parlour or living room (toward the front) and a modest store room (toward the rear); on the other side are two bedrooms. There is no separate dining room. The hall leads directly to a rear extension that is accessed down two steps. Here there is a kitchen, small pantry, and equally small bedroom (perhaps for a servant). Stairs to the cellar are squeezed into a far corner. The hierarchy is simple: the living room and two bedrooms are in the main block; the service rooms are in a back extension.[2]

Turning to individual rooms, we see that parlours (living rooms) are found in all Ontario Cottages. In smaller cottages, there is normally just one, while in larger ones there could be two. (One of Howard's cottage designs actually includes four parlours!) Other variations are the inclusion of a drawing room instead of a parlour and the inclusion of both a drawing room and a parlour. Although parlours were sometimes called "sitting rooms" or "living rooms" in Howard's drawings, his provision for a drawing room, parlour, and living room in one cottage design reflects a descending order of formality, with the drawing room being the most formal and the living room the least.

Dining rooms are usually located on the main floor, and frequently to the left as one

Inside 157

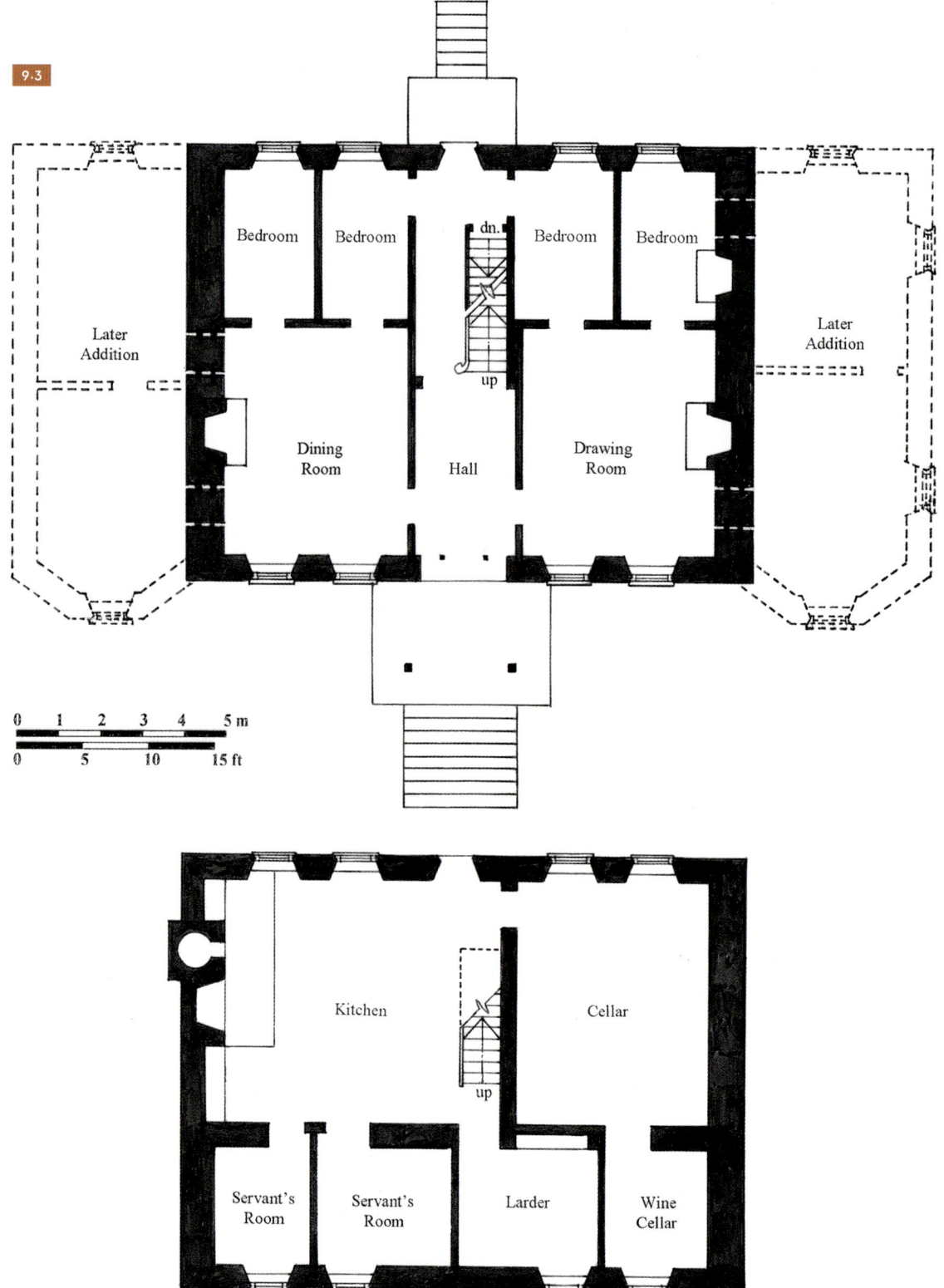

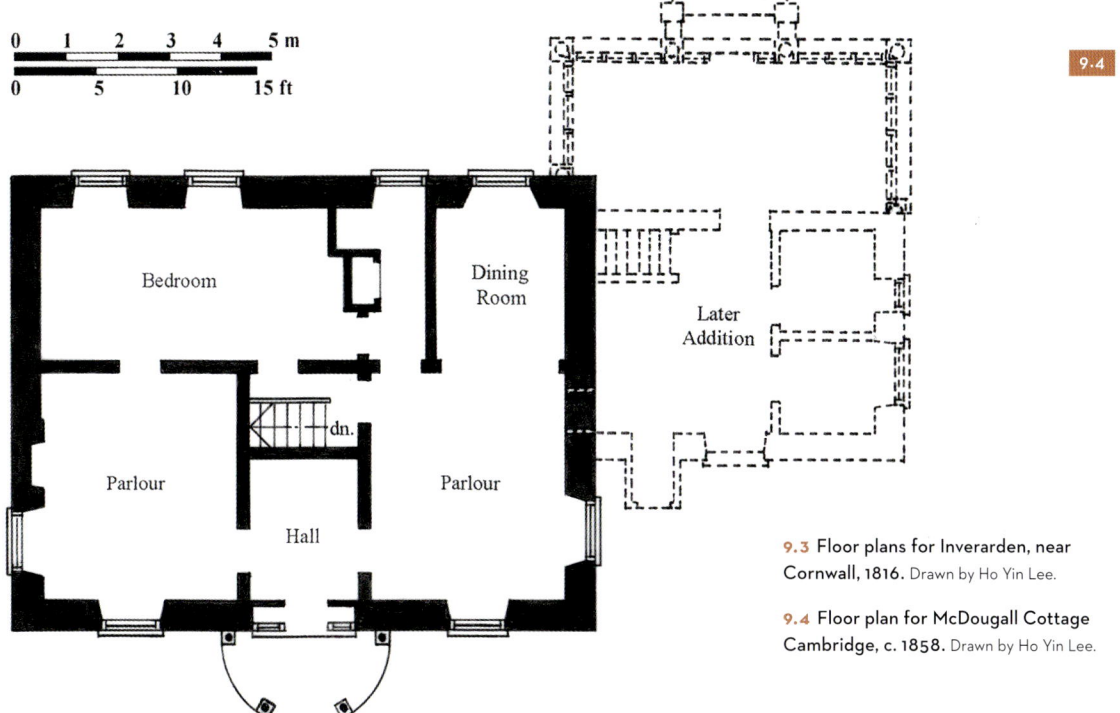

9.3 Floor plans for Inverarden, near Cornwall, 1816. Drawn by Ho Yin Lee.

9.4 Floor plan for McDougall Cottage Cambridge, c. 1858. Drawn by Ho Yin Lee.

enters. Perhaps surprisingly, in some grander cottages the dining room was originally located in the basement near the kitchen, as in Butler House (c. 1817) in Niagara-on-the-Lake (PLATE 2.1), Woodburn (1834) in Beamsville (PLATE 6.9), and Woodale (1846) in Dundas (PLATE 9.1). In all these examples, however, the basement is raised, with sizable windows providing generous light.

As this chapter's epigraph makes clear, placing kitchens and their related rooms in the basement was not uncommon in early cottages. By confining kitchen activities to the basement, the heat from cooking was made more bearable during the warmer months. Inverarden, an 1816 Regency Cottage near Cornwall, has a basement kitchen (FIG. 9.3 + PLATE 9.2). Some cottages have both winter and summer kitchens—the winter kitchen in the basement and the summer kitchen in an attached ell, at either the back or the side of the house. More typical is the simple migration of the basement kitchen to a newer kitchen ell. In Cambridge, for example, a kitchen ell was added to the south side of McDougall Cottage (c. 1858) about ten years after it was built (FIG. 9.4 + PLATES 9.3 + 9.4). In St. Marys, a kitchen ell was added to the rear of Windrush Cottage (1870), also about a decade later (FIG. 9.5 + PLATE 9.5).

Putting the kitchen in the basement, along with other rooms, is also logical for sites with major changes in elevation. Near St. Marys, the land falls away on the south side

Inside

9.5

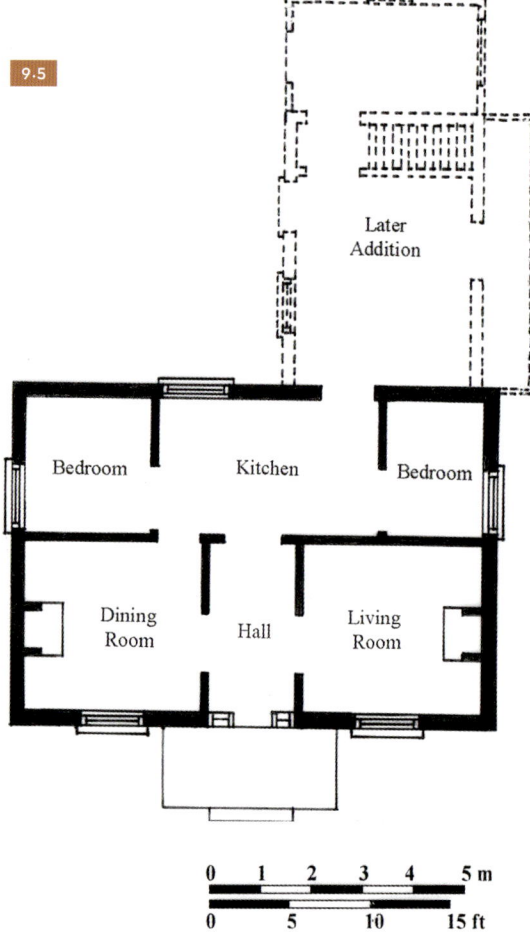

9.5 Floor plan for Windrush Cottage, St. Marys, 1870. Drawn by Ho Yin Lee.

9.6 Floor plan for Drew Cottage, Woodstock, 1833. Drawn by Ho Yin Lee.

of Wood–Simpson House (c. 1856), revealing a two-storey structure (PLATE 6.16). Here an exterior door gives direct access to the old kitchen, and good-sized windows provide adequate light. In Port Hope, a town riddled with ravines, seemingly one-storey cottages frequently become two storeys at the rear. Other examples include the Cassels Road East cottage (c. 1845) in Brooklin (PLATE 9.6) and the Main Street cottage (1840s) in Newburgh (PLATE 9.7).

But the kitchen is not relegated to the basement or an attached ell in all cases. The extensive Drew Cottage (1833) in Woodstock included the kitchen under its ample hipped roof, though it was clearly segregated from the "best" rooms and placed at the back (with smaller chambers, likely bedrooms, on either side) (FIG. 9.6 + PLATE 2.4).

Last but not least are the bedrooms, among the most private parts of a house. Normally called "chambers," they varied in size and placement. In some houses, including Drew Cottage, there is a clear hierarchy between what was then called the "best bed room" and the smaller bedrooms, some of which were tucked up under the eaves and presumably meant for servants. In Inverarden, narrow slip bedrooms are found on the main floor, directly off the parlour and the dining room.

No matter the type of layout or the number and distribution of rooms, the most compelling qualities of the cottage plan are evident: its centralizing nature and compactness.

9.6

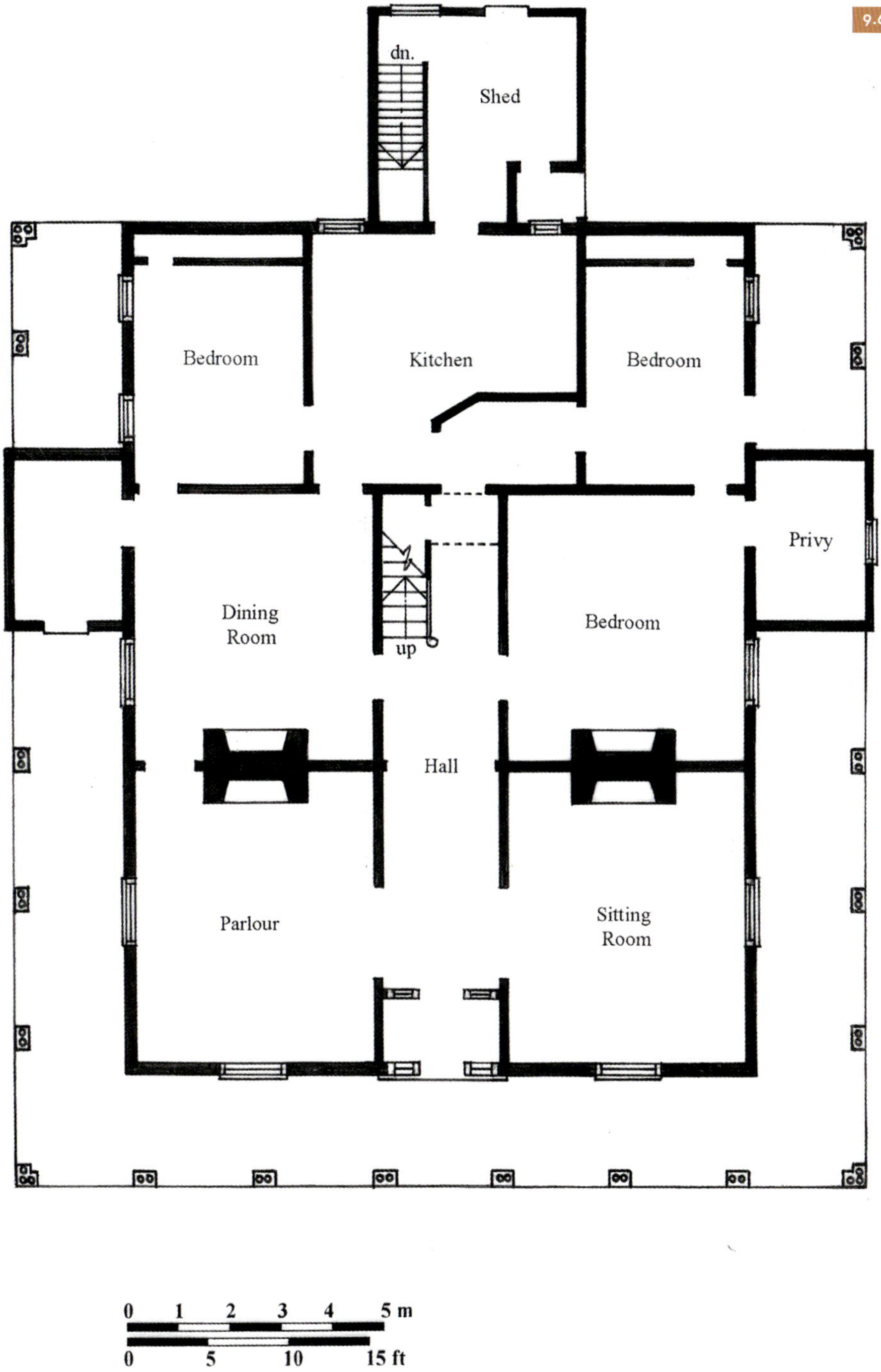

dn.
Shed
Bedroom
Kitchen
Bedroom
Privy
Dining Room
up
Bedroom
Hall
Parlour
Sitting Room
0 1 2 3 4 5 m
0 5 10 15 ft

PLATE 9.1
Woodale

Cross Street,
Dundas, 1846

PLATE 9.2
Inverarden

Montreal Road, near Cornwall, 1816

PLATE 9.3

McDougall Cottage

Grand Avenue South,
Cambridge (Galt), c. 1858

PLATE 9.4

McDougall Cottage

Grand Avenue South, Cambridge (Galt), c. 1858

PLATE 9.5
Windrush Cottage
Robinson Street,
St. Marys, 1870

PLATE 9.6
Cassels Road East, Brooklin, c. 1845

PLATE 9.7
Main Street,
Newburgh, 1840s

Inhabiting the Ontario Cottage

10

> The house has a simple but impressive grandeur. There is a sense of harmony and balance in the design elements. The several large window openings are positioned so you feel you are living as one with the outdoor landscape. Facing south/southwest, we see the sunrise over nearby Kempenfelt Bay, and the sunset in the west. It makes me feel safe and at peace.
> **SU MURDOCH**, note to Dan Schneider

THOSE WHO LIVE IN A PLACE have a special perspective on it, of course. They experience it all the time as part of daily life. So who better to tell us about the Ontario Cottage than its inhabitants, who see it as much from the inside as out, and for whom it is not just a building but a home? We talked to some of them about what first drew them to their Ontario Cottage, how it makes them feel, and the special things about it.

For Derrick, who shares a late Victorian cottage in St. Thomas (PLATE 3.12) with his partner, Ron, the Ontario Cottage is "the Ontario vernacular" and "just Ontario to me."[1] The couple were looking for a place in 1986, and the small brick house in an older neighbourhood was the first one they looked at. "We fell in love with it right away," Derrick says.

The immediate, almost visceral appeal of the cottage is a common chord in "first impression" stories. Dan wasn't even in the market for a home when, on a drive near St. Marys in 1990, he spotted an abandoned stone Ontario Cottage on a hill (PLATE 6.16).[2] "Wow," he thought, and stopped to investigate.

10.1 Front and west facades of Su's cottage, Barrie, c. 1880. Photograph from *Beautiful Barrie: The City and Its People* (Barrie: DBS Heritage Consulting & Communications, 2005), 69. Courtesy of Su Murdoch, B.E.S. Rudachyk, and K.H. Schick.

A few months later, on his first day as a tenant of the property, Dan wrote in his diary,

> The place is a dump, but I love it. It has such a quiet dignity and presence even in its forlorn state. The potential of the house and landscape are incredible.[3]

In Barrie, Su and her husband, Harry, despite their real estate agent's skepticism ("Are you sure?"), put in an offer on an early frame cottage in 1980.[4] That house too had seen better days (FIG. 10.1). Asked what attracted them to the house, Su says,

> Even in its derelict state, most of the original trim, panelled doors, builder's hardware, flooring, window sashes, front doorcase with sidelights and transom, twelve-foot ceilings, wood cornice, etc. were in near original condition. It was a deserving candidate for restoration/revitalization.[5]

The modest nature of most cottages is clearly part of their charm. When Larry and his wife, Catherine, acquired their yellow brick house, Windrush Cottage, overlooking the Thames River in St. Marys (PLATE 9.5), in 1981, its "smallness" was part of the appeal.[6] "It wasn't a great big grand house," says Catherine. Ontario Cottages, she adds, "do show that you can have interesting, lovely spaces to live in that are small-scale."

Along with scale, Larry highlights the importance of proportion (see chapter 5): "When people say, 'Why is [your house] so nice?,' well, it has very good proportions." He points out that, for the main block of the building, the ratio of length across the front to depth to height of the walls is 3:2:1. The point about proportion applies inside too. "It may be something you appreciate more the more you live in it," says Catherine, noting that their front room is almost a cube: twelve feet by twelve feet, with almost twelve-foot ceilings.

Back in Barrie, Su, sitting in her large, square front room, which has a similarly high ceiling, talks about a "feel of balance," where "everything is in ratio." "You feel that in this room," she says, recounting how visitors to the house often inexplicably wander about

"feeling the room." The story underlines how subtle yet irresistible the pull of good proportions—a kind of beauty, after all—can be.

In Port Hope, Malcolm, the owner of a semi-attached brick cottage, part of Robert Youdan Terrace (PLATE 10.1), confesses, "Before I moved here, I didn't know what an Ontario Cottage was."[7] But he soon learned that Port Hope, with its outstanding collection of Ontario Cottages in a range of styles, was "a mecca for them." Malcolm too appreciates the high ceilings and relatively big rooms but emphasizes the "warm, welcoming sensation" of his house, which he called "a refuge—quiet, cozy." To the question of how he came to live there, he answered simply, "Serendipity."

About her brick cottage in Southampton that she left decades ago but still pines for, Lynda says, "I absolutely loved that house, wide plank floors, large principal rooms, high ceilings, very quiet and I felt as though I belonged there."[8] As a memento of her time there, her brother, artist Greg Curnoe, did a watercolour of the house on his sketchpad the day she moved out (FIG. 10.2).

Says Su,

This and other early examples [of Ontario Cottages] I have experienced invariably give me a sense of being wrapped and soothed by the house. I often wonder if the low hipped roof and deep eaves are like a protective umbrella. Most have

windows that frame outside vistas, drawing you into the peace of nature.[9]

This feeling of "being wrapped" by the cottage, of feeling "safe and at peace" (Su again), appears to be particularly connected to the distinctive hipped roof, with its usually deep eaves. What Vitruvius likened to the hard shell of a turtle (see chapter 7), the Ontario Cottage roof has also been compared to a "tea caddy" (Catherine), a "kind of toque" (Dan), and a "protective umbrella" (Su).

Related to its protective, low-exposure profile, Larry and Catherine see the Ontario Cottage roof as having a "natural," self-effacing quality, unlike the "show-off" roofs of many grander (old and even contemporary) houses that have "gables everywhere." Catherine notes that this gives more prominence to the facades of the building and their typically strong symmetry.

For Malcolm, whose house shares a hipped roof with the house next door, the roof means a special connection with his neighbour: "If

10.2 Greg Curnoe (1936–1992), *Moving Out, Southampton*, 1973, watercolour on paper, 8¼ × 10⅔ inches. Courtesy of The Estate of Greg Curnoe.

we have to do any [roof] projects, it's usually a combined event, so having fantastic neighbours makes a big difference." He jokes that it's a case of "being joined at the hip here," figuratively and literally.

If the roof is the cap on the cottage, the windows are its eyes and the portal to its surroundings and the outside world. Dan appreciates the outside symmetry of his farmhouse cottage—not just the three-bay front facade (with a window on either side of the door) but also the side facades, each with two main-floor windows identically placed. And it is the result of this placement combined with the symmetry inside the house that enchants him: the side windows of the two main rooms on either side of the centre hall line up with each other, and because the doors to those rooms also line up on the same axis, one can see straight through the house from one side to the other and out the windows to the landscape. (See FIG. 9.4 for an example of this type of plan.)

Larry and Catherine speak of the importance of their windows in providing light on four sides: the windows are large, and "the size of the windows for the dimensions of the house ... mean that we've always had a sense of light in the house—light and views." (Larry notes that the relatively large windows for a house of its size "tend to make the structure look much smaller than it actually is: architectural historians refer to this as 'miniaturization.'")

Of course, old windows also involve work, especially if wooden storm sashes are involved. Derrick remarks, "We are probably the last people on the block who put [storm windows] up in the fall and take them down in the spring." But even after more than thirty years, he sees it not as a chore but as a seasonal ritual. In autumn, he says with a laugh, "You feel very cozy once they're up, even though the house is quite cold and drafty."

As for verandas, some cottages (Malcolm's, Derrick's, Lynda's former house) have them; some (Su's, Larry and Catherine's, Dan's) don't, originally having just a stoop or small porch at the entrance. Catherine points out that, for country folk at the time, it would have been expensive to build a veranda, with verandas maybe even thought of as a "stupid

10.3 Denis Héroux, pen-and-ink on paper, 1999. The drawing shows Dan's cottage from the approximate location where he first glimpsed it in 1990. Courtesy of Dan Schneider.

luxury." Dan agrees and hazards that "farm or rural cottages seem much less likely to have verandas than cottages in towns," where people might have had "more leisure time for veranda-sitting, not to mention neighbours to watch."

Unlike Ontario Cottages in urban locations, however, country cottages by definition were isolated; their owners and builders would have had more discretion as to the siting of the house. We may wonder what conscious picturesque notions went into the choice of a building's location by practical people, or whether it just seemed sensible to build on hills or overlooking rivers. Larry and Catherine's home was built in what was then a rural setting on the edge of St. Marys. Catherine describes its allure:

> We were very attracted to its location directly on the river and with [a] large garden to the side, and it seemed to us, in a picturesque town, one of the very picturesque spots.

As Larry sums up, "It's wonderfully set."

Dan's diary records that for him too the picturesque pull of the siting of his cottage on a hillside (FIG. 10.3) was key:

> It is an extremely lovely spot—the setting is the thing that attracted me in the first place (and the reason I found the house)—a very pastoral landscape with remarkably few modern intrusions.[10]

The corollary, which we already touched on, to the picturesque setting of a place is the views from the place to its surroundings. From Su's windows, "you feel you are living as one with the outdoor landscape," and she can see the sun rise over Kempenfelt Bay. For Catherine and Larry, "there are beautiful views from every window" of natural features and cultural landmarks, such as the Thames River, the St. Marys town hall, and Sarnia Bridge (a former railway bridge, now an elevated boardwalk). Larry jokes that a previous owner "loved showing off the view from her bathroom, which she declared was the finest [view] in St. Marys."

As with the inhabitants of many historic homes, a common trait among Ontario Cottage occupants is long tenure—and never wanting to leave. Says Derrick, "We don't intend to leave until they carry us out feet first." Lynda found the departure from her Southampton cottage, the result of a marriage breakup, wrenching and thinks of the house wistfully even after fifty years. Although he still holds onto the legal tenancy, Dan too had to give up the habitation of his cottage to others. Malcolm does not want to leave his house but concedes, "Who knows what the future will bring."

And this brings in another theme: stewardship. The future will inevitably bring other owners and occupants to take the place of those of us here now, just as we have supplanted those who came before. For a place one is so attached to, this realization inspires a compelling sense of care and responsibility for the cottage in the present. As Su says,

> I am the steward of this house and feel I have been given a gift to be a part of its continuum since [the cottage was built] in the 1840s.... We put the house, its architectural elements, its features first.... I like to think that the house has been a witness to [local historical events] and I'm just part of that continuum.... It's my responsibility to be its steward, to make sure that its integrity carries on.

Respecting the house means that changes, inevitably needed over time, are made with great care. In making what was just a part-time home into a permanent one, Larry and

Catherine recently finished a substantial rear addition.

> In 2021, a modern addition consisting of a kitchen, bedroom, two bathrooms, and entrance hall was completed.... Recycled brick closely matching the original was obtained from a demolished house near Brussels, Ontario. This brick was laid with beaded mortar, headers, compound lintels, and stone sills in an attempt to replicate the original as closely as possible. The scale and roofline, colour of the paint, wooden windows, and other features were designed and chosen to match the original fabric of the 1870 house, viz, to make the two indivisible.[11]

This careful stewardship extends not just to the fabric of the cottage—the bricks and mortar—but also to the more intangible history and stories of the house. Sometimes recorded, sometimes not (and sometimes not even true), these stories help convey the feeling of continuum that Su talks about. Dan tells a great tale of a young farmer, the farmer's sister, and a hired man who lived together in his house in the 1930s: "The story goes that the farmer died in the barn, apparently from being kicked by a horse; but some say the horse was two-legged. The sister and the hired man carried on."

The desire to steward and protect a cottage may also motivate its owner to seek legal protection for the property through heritage designation. While most of the Ontario Cottages discussed in this chapter are designated by the local municipality, a few, like Derrick and Ron's house in St. Thomas, are not. Derrick recalls that they were interested in designation status decades ago when there was a provincial incentive program to help with repairs, but the idea was promptly dismissed by the head of the local heritage committee on the grounds, according to Derrick, that "nobody important ever lived there." To this day, Derrick wears the slight like a badge of honour, saying jokingly, "Nobody important ever lived here then—and nobody important lives here now."

PLATE 10.1
Robert Youdan Terrace

Baldwin Street,
Port Hope, c. 1853

CONCLUSION

THE ONTARIO COTTAGE, a form almost instantly recognizable in the province's rural, small-town, and urban landscapes, has a noble pedigree. Its boxy shape and trademark hipped roof may be traced all the way back to the Palladian villa. In its adopted province, as we've seen, the Ontario Cottage has proven very adaptable to the situation and the times—chameleon-like, it can be smaller or larger; have walls of wood, stone, or brick; don a centre gable or veranda or kitchen ell or none at all; fit on a town lot or take advantage of a picturesque setting. Perhaps most obvious are the different stylistic accoutrements that have dressed up its core form, be these neoclassical, Gothic, or some eclectic combination.

However the Ontario Cottage is fitted out, its appeal is at the same time immediate and subtle. We have identified the building's key characteristics and analyzed the ratios in its proportions, but there are intangible things at play here. Sometimes "you just feel it," as one Ontario Cottage occupant said of the effect of a particular, well-proportioned room. "Each time we approach the cottage," said another, "we catch our breath."[1] Beyond feelings of pleasure for the harmonious—or even of awe for the beautiful—something more primordial may be going on: an affinity between the archetypal Ontario Cottage and deep human instincts about house and home.

All of this is what makes the Ontario Cottage perfect of its kind.

We do not know how many Ontario Cottages were built in Ontario in the twelve or so decades after 1800. Thousands, certainly; perhaps, at a guess, ten to fifteen thousand or more. While countless cottages will have been lost over the years, mainly to redevelopment in towns and cities, with the majority of these being smaller worker's cottages, the Ontario

Cottage is far from being an endangered species. But preservation challenges continue and will likely intensify. Rural cottages, for example, have long been at risk of demolition as farms consolidate and old farmhouses become surplus to current needs. Fortunately, many Ontario Cottages, including most of those illustrated in this book, have been recognized by their communities as heritage structures and designated under the Ontario Heritage Act, either individually or as part of heritage conservation districts.

But in this book, a case is made for the wider significance of the Ontario Cottage, a significance to Ontario as a whole. Here we have a foreign (British) houseform that was exported to Canada and was so well assimilated to its adopted land (Upper Canada, now Ontario) that it has become part of the Ontario vernacular. This has happened nowhere else in Canada. The Ontario Cottage—collectively, as a building type—deserves to be recognized and celebrated as a distinctive heritage feature of the province.

If this book helps raise awareness of the cultural significance of the Ontario Cottage—singly, as part of its neighbourhood or surroundings, and as an element of what makes Ontario and its landscape unique—it will have served its objective.

ACKNOWLEDGEMENTS

FIGURE 1
Steve Cameron, associate publisher + vice president
Stephanie Fysh, proofreader
Judy Phillips, copy editor
Mark Redmayne, publicity director
Mélanie Ritchot, marketing coordinator
Lara Smith, managing editor
Jessica Sullivan, designer
Heidi Waechtler, sales director

ARCHIVES, LIBRARIES, AND MUSEUMS
Archives and Special Collections, Western Libraries, Western University
Archives of Ontario
Library and Archives Canada
Museum London
Norfolk County Archives
Special Collections, Toronto Reference Library
Stratford-Perth Archives
Thomas Fisher Rare Book Library, University of Toronto
Woodstock Museum

INDIVIDUALS
Those who helped with various aspects of the project, especially with fundraising, research, and finding just the right research direction

Mike Baker
Matthew Blackett
Fred Cane
Katie Cummer
Lynda Curnoe
Joe DiStefano
Jean Hung (Archives and Special Collections, Western Libraries)
Joan King and Bruce McBain
Joshua Klar (Norfolk County Archives)
Abe and the late Gay Langdon
Megan Lockhart (Stratford-Perth Archives)
John Lorinc
Linda and John Luciani
Michael McClelland (ERA Architects)
Mary McCoy
Harvey McCue
Jennifer McKendry
Chloe Montpetit (Archives of Ontario)
Su Murdoch
The late Stephen A. Otto
Catherine and Larry Pfaff
The late and unforgettable Edward Phelps
Malcolm Pike

Adam Pollard (Woodstock Museum)
Carol Priamo
Andrew Pruss (ERA Architects)
Theresa Regnier (Archives and Special Collections, Western Libraries)
Catherine Riddell (ERA Architects)
Quinn Robinson (Library and Archives Canada)
John Rutledge
Rebecca Sciarra (ASI)
Sandra Shaul
Meredith Stewart (ASI)
Nancy Tausky
Lorraine Tinsley
G.E. (Ted) Williams

And multiple thanks to the owners of Ontario Cottages, who welcomed us into their homes and shared their stories, and to Ontario's dedicated Local Architectural Conservation Advisory Committees (LACACs), precursors to today's Municipal Heritage Committees, which helped facilitate our research efforts in so many ways.

And thanks also to those who we have inadvertently forgotten to acknowledge. This project does have a long time span…

FUNDING
Individuals and companies that donated funds to make this book possible

John Ambrose and Eugenia Venchiarutti
Anonymous
Tamara Anson-Cartwright
ARA
ASI
Martine Celej
DJ McRae Heritage Restoration
Donald Schmitt Architects
ERA Architects
GBCA
Don Holland
Paul R. King
Bruce Kuwabara
Karen Lang
Craig Machel
Ian B. Maclennan
The late John H. Moore
Audrey and Dipak Rastogi
Lynn Schneider and Jim Raglan
Taylor Hazell Architects

Government funding
Canada Council
Department of Canadian Heritage Museums Assistance Programme
Ontario Arts Council

CONTRIBUTORS

LYNNE D. DISTEFANO, PhD (UPenn), is a specialist in cultural heritage and urban conservation. Co-founder and past director of the University of Hong Kong's Architectural Conservation Programmes, she is an adjunct professor at the university and a faculty associate at the Willowbank School of Restoration Arts. From 2006 to 2018, Lynne was an ICOMOS expert and technical evaluator for UNESCO World Heritage sites in Austria, China, Japan, Laos, the Philippines, and South Korea. Previously, Lynne was a chief curator at Museum London and an associate professor at Brescia University College, Western University. Lynne has served on the board of directors of the Ontario Heritage Foundation (now Trust) at two different times and on Heritage Toronto's Programme Committee. She is the co-author (with Nancy Z. Tausky) of *Victorian Architecture in London and Southwestern Ontario: Symbols of Aspiration* and (with Ho Yin Lee) has written a number of books and articles about cultural heritage in Hong Kong. In 2025 (with Lavina Ahuja), she completed the editing of the second of two books on adaptive reuse in Asia. Lynne lives in Toronto's Annex, where she sits on the Annex Residents' Association's Heritage Committee and Planning and Development Committee. From the 17th floor of her condo, she dreams of living in an Ontario Cottage.

DAN SCHNEIDER is a heritage enthusiast, policy wonk, writer, and professional heritage consultant. A lawyer by training, Dan has been active in the cultural heritage field for forty-five years. Formerly a senior policy advisor with Ontario's culture ministry, he was lead policy expert on many government heritage initiatives, including comprehensive changes to the Ontario Heritage Act in 2005. Now based in St. Marys, Ontario, Dan is principal of Dan Schneider Heritage Consulting. His heritage policy blog *OHA+M* was founded in 2015 and is housed on the website of the Heritage Resources Centre of the University of Waterloo. Boasting 125 (and counting) articles on a wide range of issues, the blog is widely consulted and has won two awards, including a 2017 award from the Canadian Association of Heritage Professionals. As a volunteer, Dan is also a long-time member of Architectural

Conservancy Ontario (ACO) and chairs ACO's policy committee. He is a founding member of the Stratford-Perth County ACO branch and currently serves as its president. Previously, Dan has been appointed to the St. Marys municipal heritage committee and was a member of the town's Doors Open committee. For many decades, Dan was proud custodian of a circa 1856 limestone Ontario Cottage near St. Marys.

STEVEN EVANS is a Toronto-based photographer with forty-five years of experience developing his craft. His personal photography has been exhibited and published nationally and internationally and can be found in numerous public collections, including the Canadian Centre for Architecture, Art Gallery of Ontario, and City of Toronto Archives, as well as several private and corporate collections. In his commercial architectural photography practice, he has worked with many of Canada's top firms. His images have been published in national and international magazines and websites, and his work has been honoured by the National Magazine Awards. Evans has also taught and lectured at Toronto Metropolitan University. His most recent project was the documentation of Ontario Place in Toronto, which culminated in a book and exhibition in 2023 entitled *As It Is: A Precarious Moment in the Life of Ontario Place*.

HO YIN LEE, PhD (HKU) is an architect, well-published academic, and experienced practitioner in built-heritage conservation. He is the co-founder and past director of the University of Hong Kong's Architectural Conservation Programmes. Ho Yin has been appointed by government agencies in Hong Kong, mainland China, and overseas as an expert advisor or a consultant for conservation projects. He has also been appointed to numerous heritage conservation statutory boards and committees in Hong Kong, including the Hong Kong Government's Antiquities Advisory Board and Urban Renewal Authority Board of Directors (as non-executive director).

NOTES

1 DEFINING THE ONTARIO COTTAGE

Farm Architecture, *Canada Farmer* 1, no. 2 (February 1, 1864): 20.

1. *The Canada Farmer* was published from 1864 to 1876. Issues sometimes contained plans and elevations for houses considered appropriate for rural areas. See https://www.canadiana.ca/view/oocihm.8_04206. Although the journal was intended for farmers, both its readership and the extent of its rural influence remain unclear. After its brief run, the publication merged with *The Globe* to become *The Globe and Canada Farmer*.
2. Labels in the reproduced illustrations reflect the original casing.
3. As argued by Henry Glassie, a noted twentieth-century anthropologist, deviations can be explained by applying the principles of structural linguistics. American scholar Camille Wells credits Glassie for solving, in his 1975 study *Folk Housing in Middle Virginia: A Structural Analysis of Historic Artifacts*, "the problems presented by individual deviation from ... ideal templates by applying the principles of structural linguistics." Glassie argues that, essentially, "every house is composed of distinct geometric components that are linked and integrated according to generally accepted rules of architectural 'grammar.' In this way, it is possible to explain the variety as well as the similarity that exists among the houses of a particular time and place." Camille Wells, "Old Claims and New Demands: Vernacular Architecture Studies Today," *Perspectives in Vernacular Architecture* 2 (1986): 2.
4. "Vernacular architecture" refers to buildings that use regional forms and materials.
5. See R.W. Brunskill's *Illustrated Handbook of Vernacular Architecture*, 3rd ed. (London: Faber and Faber, 1987), 74. Brunskill looks at walling, roofing, plans and sections, and architectural details, as well as at different types of vernacular buildings. In regard to roofing, he identifies five variations of what he calls the "hipped roof family": the hipped roof; the gablet roof; the hipped roof on a projection; the hipped gambrel (mansard) roof; and the hipped M-shaped roof.
6. Darrell A. Norris, "Vetting the Vernacular: Local Varieties in Ontario's Housing," *Ontario History* 74, no. 2 (June 1982): 74.
7. Thomas F. McIlwraith, *Looking for Old Ontario: Two Centuries of Landscape Change* (Toronto, University of Toronto Press, 1997), 106, 110–12.
8. Marion MacRae and Anthony Adamson, *The Ancestral Roof: Domestic Architecture of Upper Canada* (Toronto: Clarke, Irwin, 1963), 240.
9. Ibid., 77. MacRae and Adamson describe the "flimsy" summer cottage, "in which Ontario keeps holiday," as "a modified, specialized descendant" of the Regency Cottage.
10. *The Oxford English Dictionary*, rev. ed. (1978), under "cottage."

11. Quoted in Daniel Maudlin, *The Idea of the Cottage in English Architecture, 1760–1860* (London: Routledge, 2015), 2. In his introduction (1–16), Maudlin gives an excellent overview of the architect-designed cottage, which was seen as "the embodiment of the ideal of rural retreat" (1, 2) and an art object to be viewed within a landscape (see page 2). Also, Maudlin identifies four types of architect-designed cottages: the first three are associated with country estates (retreat, labourer's cottage, and gatehouse), and the fourth is the cottage-villa (6).
12. According to Peter Ennals and Deryck W. Holdsworth in *Homeplace: The Making of the Canadian Dwelling over Three Centuries* (Toronto: University of Toronto Press, 1998), 46, in the 1810s (during the Regency period), current styles were adapted to smaller houses, which were referred to as "cottages" or "villas." As mentioned in note 11 above, Maudlin identifies the cottage-villa as one of the four types of cottages.
13. John Plaw, *Sketches for Country Houses, Villas, and Rural Dwellings [...]* (London: J. Taylor, 1800), 11 and plate VII. This architectural pattern book is one of a number of such building guides produced during the late eighteenth and nineteenth centuries. These books provide building plans—or plans for parts of buildings, such as doors and windows—frequently with lengthy descriptions, and sometimes with detailed instructions.
14. The bungalow's plan can sometimes be asymmetrical; its roof, not always hipped, tends to be lower and has noticeably broad eaves; its veranda, when it has one, is frequently found only at the front, covered by the extension of the main roof; and its windows can be clustered. Materials, too, are used differently. At times, the bungalow possesses a ruggedness in its use of randomly laid facing stones and exposed structural members, particularly at the eaves.
15. John Woodforde, *The Truth about Cottages: A History and an Illustrated Guide to 50 Types of English Cottage* (London: I.B. Tauris, 2007), 7.
16. In this sense, the cottage can be seen as an example of the idea of complementarity. This is the concept that "one single thing, when considered from different perspectives, can be seen to have very different or even contradictory properties," according to Frank Wilczek, as quoted in Nell Freudenberger, "Electrons, Photons, Gluons, Quarks," *New York Times*, February 8, 2021, Book Review, 15. Wilczek is a Nobel-winning physicist. Complementarity is explored in chapter 10 of his *Fundamentals: Ten Keys to Reality* (New York: Penguin Press, 2021).

2 A BIRD'S-EYE VIEW

Randall White, *Ontario, 1610–1985: A Political and Economic History* (Toronto: Dundurn Press, 1985), 148.

1. Properties illustrated in the county atlases may not be representative, as property owners underwrote publication costs.
2. City and Vicinity, *London Advertiser*, November 25, 1873, 3.
3. Ibid.
4. The authors are grateful to Rebecca Sciarra and Meredith Stewart at ASI for this information.

3 TRADITION AND STYLE

James Malton, *An Essay on British Cottage Architecture [...]* (London: Hookham and Carpenter, 1798), 7.

1. For an excellent overview of the work of Palladio, see James S. Ackerman, *Palladio* (London: Penguin Books, 1966). Nathalie Clerk, in *Palladian Style in Canadian Architecture* (Hull, PQ: National

Historic Parks and Sites Branch, Parks Canada, Environment Canada, 1984), 7–8, makes a compelling argument for using the Palladian label rather than the Georgian.
2. Vitruvius, *The Ten Books on Architecture*, trans. Morris Hicky Morgan, bk. 1, *The Fundamental Principles of Architecture* (Cambridge, MA: Harvard University Press, 1914; repr., New York: Dover Publications, 1960), 13.
3. Ibid., 13–16.
4. Nathalie Clerk, in *Palladian Style in Canadian Architecture*, 9–13, gives a detailed account of Palladio's magnum opus and related publications.
5. Ackerman, *Palladio*, 19.
6. Clerk, *Palladian Style*, 9–10.
7. Cyril M. Harris, ed., *Historic Architecture Sourcebook* (New York: McGraw-Hill, 1977), 431.
8. Andrea Palladio, *The Four Books of Architecture*, trans. Robert Tavernor and Richard Schofield (Cambridge, MA: MIT Press, 1997), 147.
9. Leslie Maitland, in *Neoclassical Architecture in Canada* (Hull, PQ: National Historic Parks and Sites Branch, Parks Canada, Environment Canada, 1984), 20–31, provides a clear understanding of the three phases of neoclassicism.
10. "Tracery" refers to "curvilinear openwork shapes" that form a decorative pattern, as in the upper part of a door or window. Harris, *Historic Architecture Sourcebook*, 544.
11. Ibid., 157, 180, 410.
12. For some mid- to late-nineteenth-century cottages, the gable (pediment) over the centrally placed door is sharply angled, almost pinched. This squeezed form reflects the reduced dimensions of more modest cottages. The bays on either side of the centrally placed door are smaller, and the width of the doorway is correspondingly reduced.
13. In Canada, the first stage of the Gothic Revival is the Romantic Gothic Revival, where Gothic details are applied to otherwise Palladian-inspired buildings. See Mathilde Brosseau, *Gothic Revival in Canadian Architecture* (Ottawa: Minister of Supply and Services Canada, 1980), 8–12.
14. High Victorian Gothic is the third stage of the Gothic Revival in Canada. It follows the Rationalistic and Ecclesiological Gothic Revival (the second stage) and is characterized by a creative mix of Gothic styles (eclectic); contrasting colours, materials, and textures; and marked asymmetry in both plan and elevation (picturesque). Ibid., 20–26.
15. For the reference to fifteenth-century Elizabethan architecture, see Harris, *Historic Architecture Sourcebook*, 442. The quotation is from Leslie Maitland, Jacqueline Hucker, and Shannon Ricketts, *A Guide to Canadian Architectural Styles* (Peterborough, ON: Broadview Press, 1992), 98.
16. J.C. Loudon, *An Encyclopaedia of Cottage, Farm, and Villa Architecture and Furniture […]* (London: Longman, Orme, Brown, Green, and Longmans, 1839), 102.

4 DESIGN SOURCES

George Eliot, *Middlemarch* (London: Harper Press, 2011), 31.
1. For an understanding of the reference to Lazarus, see Luke 16:20 AV: "And there was a certain beggar named Lazarus, which was laid at his [a certain rich man's] gate, full of sores."
2. Michael McMordie, "Picturesque Pattern Books and Pre-Victorian Designers," *Architectural History* 18 (1975): 43–59. This article considers more than sixty illustrated books offering designs for cottages and larger houses. The major period for such publications is from 1790 to 1835, coinciding with the first streams of emigrants from Great Britain to Upper Canada.
3. For an understanding of the popularity of lodges,

see J.A.K. Dean, *The Gate Lodges of Ulster: A Gazetteer* (Belfast: Ulster Architectural Heritage Society, 1994). The gazetteer includes close to fifteen hundred examples of lodges spread across nine counties in today's Northern Ireland. Tim Mowl and Brian Earnshaw's *Trumpet at a Distant Gate: The Lodge as Prelude to the Country House* (London: Waterstone, 1985) is also instructive on the topic.

4. "Pyramidal" refers to Brunskill's hipped roof on a projection. We look at the types of hipped roofs in chapter 7.

5. The *Encyclopaedia,* which was updated and reissued frequently, offers an astonishing fifty designs for cottages, including one for a prefabricated cottage. J.C. Loudon, *An Encyclopaedia of Cottage, Farm, and Villa Architecture and Furniture [...]* (London: Longman, Orme, Brown, Green, and Longmans, 1839).

6. Wood is not the first person to offer cottage designs for labourers, but his detailed designs (elevations) are in contrast to the simpler designs (elevations) embedded in Nathaniel Kent's *Hints to Gentlemen of Landed Property* (London: printed for J. Dodsley, 1775). Of particular relevance to this book, in the next-to-last chapter, entitled "Reflections on the Great Importance of Cottages," Kent remarks that larger cottage roofs are to be hipped at the ends to save bricks from being used for the "peaks." Kent, *Hints to Gentlemen*, 244–45. We examine the hipped roof in detail in chapter 7.

7. John Wood, *A Series of Plans for Cottages or Habitations of the Labourer [...]*, rev. ed. (London: Architectural Library, 1806), n.p.

8. William Barber, *Farm Buildings [...]* (London: printed by John Tyler, after 1802), 1, 2.

9. Ibid., 4.

10. Arthur C. Taylor, *Designs for Agricultural Buildings Suited to Irish Estates [...]* (Dublin: Grant and Bolton, 1841), 5.

11. The cottage, as detailed in the book's plate XIII, is an ample 34 feet wide by 28 feet deep, and contains a parlour, kitchen, and three bedrooms (two of which are "slip" bedrooms). The sophistication of the design belies the "Farm House" label and suggests that the author is intent on providing designs that are more than simply utilitarian. The design reflects the persistence of the neoclassical long after the end of the Regency era—and reminds us that our earliest Ontario Cottages can also be called Regency Cottages. Ibid., n.p.

12. In England, "cottage orné" refers to "rural residences of small and humble appearance occupied by persons of refined manners and habits." Janet Wright, *Architecture of the Picturesque in Canada* (Ottawa: National Historic Parks and Sites Branch, Parks Canada, Environment Canada, 1984), 45.

13. Charles Middleton, *Picturesque and Architectural Views for Cottages, Farm Houses, and Country Villas* (Farnborough, UK: Gregg International, 1972), n.p. First printed 1793 (London).

14. A case in point is the noted proponent of the Picturesque Richard Payne Knight, who relinquished his large and fanciful Downton Castle in Shropshire, England, in the 1780s and retired to a small cottage on his estate, which he referred to fondly as "my little domestic dell." John Betjeman, "Introduction," in Tony Evans and Candida Lycett Green, *English Cottages* (Harmondsworth, UK: Penguin Books, 1984), 16.

15. John Plaw, *Sketches for Country Houses, Villas, and Rural Dwellings [...]* (London: J. Taylor, 1800), plate VII; Edmund Bartell, *Hints for Picturesque Improvements in Ornamental Cottages, and Their Scenery: Including Some Observations on the Labourer and His Cottage* (London: printed

for J. Taylor, Architectural Library, 1804), n.p.
16. "From the 1830s, the publication of high quality illustrated books waned as the spread of mass journalism brought an illustrated popular press." McMordie, "Picturesque Pattern Books," 45.
17. The preference for stone construction gives buildings a distinct stolid character. In the early nineteenth century, J.C. Loudon observed in *A Treatise on Forming, Improving, and Managing Country Residences [...]* (London: Longman, Hurst, Rees, and Orme, 1806), 126–32, that the differences between the English and the Scottish cottage are practical responses to local geography and climate. In writing about the "Scots Cottage," he observes that "the peculiar forms... originated from the abundance of stones, the comparative scarcity of wood, and the severity of the climate" (129). Close to thirty years later, Loudon would describe a simple three-bay, hipped-roof stone cottage as being "in the common Scottish manner." Loudon, *A Treatise*, 36. In *Illustrated Historical Atlas of the Counties of Northumberland and Durham, Ont.* (Toronto: H. Belden, 1878), 72, a hipped-roof cottage is described as a "Lowland Cottage."
18. The designs were entered in a housing competition sponsored by the Highland Society of Scotland. As John G. Dunbar remarks in his *Architecture of Scotland*, 2nd ed. (London: B.T. Batsford, 1978), 184, "Examples of the trim, box-like little dwellings illustrated in this and other similar books of the period may still be seen in many parts of the country, disposed individually or in neat estate villages."
19. George Smith, *Essay on the Construction of Cottages Suited for the Dwellings of the Labouring Classes [...]* (Glasgow: Blackie & Son, 1834), 33.
20. Ibid., 27.
21. Bartell, *Hints for Picturesque Improvements*, 140.
22. Colborne Lodge (1837), Howard's home in Toronto's High Park (plate 6.19), demonstrates his skillful adaptation of British design to the local context. See also fig. 9.1. The authors are grateful to the late Shirley Morris and the late Stephen A. Otto for alerting us to the fact that Howard owned a copy of Loudon's *Encyclopaedia*.
23. Storm's library is held at the Thomas Fisher Rare Book Library, University of Toronto.
24. Anson Bailey Cutts, "The Old Scottish Architecture of Ontario," *Canadian Geographical Journal* 39, no. 5 (November 1949): 203.
25. A copy of the original 1821 edition of Lamond's guide is in Archives and Special Collections, Western Libraries, Western University. This fascinating narrative has also been reprinted recently in Delhi by Gyan Books. The publisher notes, "Reprinted in 2017 with the help of [the] original edition published long back (1821)." Accessed at biblio.com on April 29, 2021. Does this suggest an ongoing interest in the relationship between the cottage and bungalow as related, yet distinctive houseforms?
26. Design 1 is a simple conical-shaped structure; Design 2 is a shed-roof structure with a symmetrical facade; Design 3 is a symmetrical gable-roof cottage; and Design 4, a symmetrical hipped-roof cottage, is labelled "Log-Cottage, or Frame-House." Designs 5, 6, 7, and 8 (Figs. 4.6–4.9) are variations of Design 4. Designs 6 and 8 draw on the period's fondness for rusticity in their use of rustic columns. The former design has two rather Baroque-looking rustic columns, described as "two trees in their natural state," supporting the entrance portico; the latter design has rustic columns, described as "trunks of trees," supporting the projecting roof that forms the roof of the veranda. Design 9, as described in chapter 3, is the most ambitious design, relying as it does on a

three-part Palladian composition (Fig. 3.2).
27. Lamond's designs predate Loudon's 1833 cottage-rich publication by twelve years.
28. Loudon, *Encyclopaedia*, 1. Punctuation has been altered for clarity.
29. Ibid., 9.
30. Not content with providing one model, Loudon proposes several variations on the hipped-roof theme. To Design 1 he adds porch pillars, ornamental chimneys, and a parapet on the terrace. To Design 2, which is derived from Design 1, he adds a veranda, ornamental chimney pots, and "a light iron parapet to the terrace." Throughout book 1 are numerous additional model cottage designs featuring a hipped roof, but Design 1 remains among the most memorable.
31. Ibid., 73.
32. *Canada Farmer* 1, no. 1 (January 15, 1864): 8.
33. A revealing detail is that Smith mentioned that the Small Gothic Cottage could be built in brick, stone, or timber. Ibid., 21. For more on Smith, see Eric Arthur, Toronto: *No Mean City*, 3rd ed., rev. Stephen A. Otto (Toronto: University of Toronto Press, 1986), 259.
34. Ibid. We also know that John George Howard (1803–1890), another Toronto architect practising at this time, had a copy of the *Encyclopedia*.
35. Although there may be a connection between British military buildings and the Ontario Cottage, it is difficult to establish a direct influence. What we do know is that the Royal Engineers designed and built a number of hipped-roof buildings. In Toronto (then known as York), Captain Robert Pilkington of the Royal Engineers designed Government House, a symmetrical, nine-bay, hipped-roof building, as part of the garrison. Ibid., 18–20. By 1815, the Royal Engineers had constructed the Commodore's Residence, part of Point Frederick (Kingston). This five-bay, hipped-roof structure with a veranda demonstrates the Royal Engineers' familiarity with the Anglo-Indian bungalow, a houseform found throughout the former British Empire. The five-bay, hipped-roof Commissariat Office (1831) was built by the Royal Engineers as part of Fort Malden (Amherstburg), while in the late 1830s and early 1840s, several three-bay, hipped-roofed "defensible lockmaster's houses" were constructed at strategic locations along the Rideau Canal by the Royal Engineers. (See whc.unesco.org, World Heritage Centre, Description of Property, Rideau Canal nomination file 1221.) We also know that British officers and half-pay officers built or lived in hipped-roof cottages. But which sources were the most influential—military buildings, some of which are influenced by the Anglo-Indian bungalow, or the plethora of other design sources?
36. The gable-roof "cousin" was another option, but it appears not to have been as popular. Perhaps that was because of the cost of materials, as mentioned by Nathaniel Kent in *Hints to Gentlemen of Landed Property* (see note 6 above) or, more likely, the hipped roof was considered easier to build.

5 AS GOOD AS GOLD, OR A MATTER OF PROPORTION

Julia Beck, letter to Lynne DiStefano, November 13, 1998.
1. James Gibbs, *A Book of Architecture Containing Designs of Buildings and Ornament* (London: 1728), ii–iii.
2. Ibid., ii.
3. Five unique orders are associated with classical architecture: Doric, Ionic, Corinthian, Tuscan, and Composite. The first three are Greek orders; the last two, Roman. Each order has a distinctive column, which supports an equally distinctive beam-like member (entablature).

4. The golden ratio is considered especially satisfying to the eye—and may be the easiest ratio to appreciate, according to Adrian Bejan, a mechanical engineer and professor at Duke University. It is a rectangle that has an aspect (width to height) ratio of 1.618:1, which the ancient Greeks discovered to have the most visually pleasing effect in architecture. Adrian Bejan, "The Golden Ratio Predicted: Vision, Cognition and Locomotion as a Single Design in Nature," *International Journal of Design & Nature and Ecodynamics* 4, no. 2 (2009), 97–104. Builders apply this ratio easily and frequently in construction.

6 CONSTRUCTING THE ONTARIO COTTAGE

Census Report of the Canadas, 1851-2, vol. 2, as summarized in Brian Coffey, "Factors Affecting the Use of Construction Materials in Early Ontario," *Ontario History* 77 (December 1983): 101.

1. In board-and-batten siding, boards are laid vertically and the seams are covered with battens. In tongue and groove siding, boards are laid horizontally; one edge has a shaped projection (the tongue), the other edge has a slit (the groove).
2. Peter John Stokes, *Old Niagara on the Lake* (Toronto: University of Toronto Press, 1971), 128.
3. *British American Cultivator* 1, no. 5 (May 1842): 76. The authors are indebted to the late Stephen A. Otto for this reference.
4. See, for example, "No Mean City," *London Free Press*, November 23, 1891, 3.
5. Robert Lamond, *A Narrative of the Rise & Progress of Emigration, from the Counties of Lanark & Renfrew, to the New Settlements in Upper Canada, on Government Grant [...]* (Glasgow: Chalmers & Collins, 1821), 82.
6. Anson Bailey Cutts, "The Old Scottish Architecture of Ontario," *Canadian Geographical Journal* 39, no. 5 (November 1949): 204.
7. John I. Rempel, *Building with Wood and Other Aspects of Nineteenth-Century Building in Central Canada*, rev. ed. (Toronto: University of Toronto Press, 1980), 282–88.
8. Coffey, "Factors Affecting the Use of Construction Materials," 301, 308, 310, 317.
9. Terry McAdorey, letter to Lynne DiStefano, August 30, 1997.

7 THE HIPPED ROOF

Jonathan Swift, *Gulliver's Travels*, ed. Claude Rawson (Oxford: Oxford University Press, 2005), 168; first published 1726. Quoted in Alan Davenport, "Innovation in Structural Engineering—Challenges for the Future," in *Structural Engineering: History and Development*, ed. R.J.W. Milne (London: E. & F.N. Spon, 1997), 128.

1. Paul Oliver, ed., *Encyclopedia of Vernacular Architecture of the World* (Cambridge, UK: Cambridge University Press, 1998), under "hipped roof," by Howard Davis. (Note: The publication date is sometimes cited as 1997.)
2. Vitruvius, *The Ten Books on Architecture*, trans. Morris Hicky Morgan, bk. 2 (Cambridge, MA: Harvard University Press, 1914; repr., New York: Dover Publications, 1960), 39.
3. Davenport, "Innovation in Structural Engineering," 131–32.
4. This has been demonstrated by wind-turbulence expert Alan Davenport in a boundary layer wind tunnel. His tests show that "the uplift suctions on the hip roof are highest at the peak of the roof where the members and surfaces intersect and the roof is considerably strengthened. On the other hand, on the gable-ended roof, not only are the suctions higher but the maximum suctions occur along the entire length of the end gable. The end trusses must carry the brunt of the wind force particularly if the roof is cantilevered to provide

for eaves." Ibid., 131.
5. Elizabeth Vincent, *Substance and Practice: Building Technology and the Royal Engineers in Canada* (Hull, PQ: National Historic Parks and Sites Branch, Environment Canada, 1993), 95.
6. The quotation is from George Smith, *Essay on the Construction of Cottages Suited for the Dwellings of the Labouring Classes [...]* (Glasgow: Blackie & Son, 1834), 18.

8 THE VERANDA

Arundhati Roy, *The God of Small Things* (London: Flamingo, 1997), 165.

1. "Integrated" refers to a type of veranda roof. See the description in the next section, "Origins."
2. The veranda is defined as "a covered porch or balcony, extending along the outside of a building, planned for summer leisure." Cyril M. Harris, ed., *Historic Architecture Sourcebook* (New York: McGraw-Hill, 1977), 564.
3. Anthony D. King, *The Bungalow: The Production of a Global Culture*, 2nd ed. (New York: Oxford University Press, 1995), 14.
4. The quotation is from ibid., 28. The term "plinth" applies to the base of a column (or other types of vertical support), the base for a statue (or memorial), or the base of an external wall. In this quotation, the term is used in the context of a platform or base for an external wall; Harris, 424.
5. King, 30.
6. Ibid., 23–24.
7. *The Oxford English Dictionary*, rev. ed. (1978), under "veranda"; Col. Henry Yule and A.C. Burnell, *Hobson-Jobson: A Glossary of Colloquial Anglo-Indian Words and Phrases, and of Kindred Terms, Etymological, Historical, Geographical and Discursive*, ed. William Crooke, 2nd ed. (London: Routledge & Kegan Paul, 1985), 964–66. The Spanish term encompasses different kinds of porches.
8. John Buonarotti Papworth, *Rural Residences Consisting of a Series of Designs for Cottages, Decorated Cottages, Small Villas, and Other Ornamental Buildings [...]* (London: J. Diggins for R. Ackermann, 1818), 104.
9. The Royal Engineers constructed Anglo-Indian bungalows throughout the British Empire, especially in cantonments. In Kingston, Ontario, as previously noted, the now demolished Commodore's Residence (pre-1815) was a five-bay, hipped-roof building with an integrated veranda (see chap. 4, n. 35).
10. The quotation is from John Plaw, *Sketches for Country Houses, Villas, and Rural Dwellings [...]* (London: J. Taylor, 1800), 11.
11. Catharine Parr Traill, *The Backwoods of Canada*, ed. Michael A. Peterman (Ottawa: Carleton University Press, 1997), 103; first published 1836 by C. Knight (London).
12. Jeanne Minhinnick notes that "clematis, cobea and honeysuckle were grown for show and shade on the verandah posts." See Jeanne Minhinnick's *At Home in Upper Canada* (Toronto: Clarke, Irwin, 1970), 11.
13. Papworth, *Rural Residences*, 103.
14. Traill, *The Backwoods of Canada*, 103.
15. Emerald D. Fowler, "Your House and Mine: Aesthetic or Not Aesthetic?" *Rose-Belford's Canadian Monthly and National Review* 8 (June 1882): 596–97.
16. John I. Rempel, *Building with Wood and Other Aspects of Nineteenth-Century Building in Central Canada*, rev. ed. (Toronto: University of Toronto Press, 1980), 344.
17. The attachment of the articulated veranda roof to the exterior wall or walls of the building was planned in advance, as nailing boards of the

correct width and length had to be inserted into brick or stone walls—or timber beams inserted for timber-framed walls—during the construction process. The veranda, whether its roof is integrated or tacked on, is rarely an afterthought.

18. Howard Collection, drawing nos. 37–39, Special Collections, Toronto Reference Library.
19. Marion MacRae and Anthony Adamson, *The Ancestral Roof: Domestic Architecture of Upper Canada* (Toronto: Clarke, Irwin, 1963), 240.
20. Traill, *The Backwoods of Canada*, 103.
21. A.J. Downing, quoted in Minhinnick, *At Home in Upper Canada*, 16.
22. Quoted in Rev. Thomas Radcliff, ed., *Authentic Letters from Upper Canada: Including an Account of Canadian Field Sports*, with an introduction by James John Talman (Toronto: Macmillan, 1953), 47; first published 1833.

9 INSIDE

The Middlesex Prototype (London), October 18, 1854.

1. Howard Collection, drawing nos. 37–39, Special Collections, Toronto Reference Library.
2. Farm Architecture, *Canada Farmer* 1, no. 2 (February 1, 1864): 20.

10 INHABITING THE ONTARIO COTTAGE

Su Murdoch, note to Dan Schneider, September 30, 2024.

1. Derrick, interview by Dan Schneider, October 8, 2024. Names have been changed for privacy reasons.
2. Dan Schneider, one of this book's authors.
3. Dan Schneider, diary entry, June 23, 1990.
4. Su Murdoch, interview by Dan Schneider, October 1, 2024.
5. Su Murdoch, note to Dan Schneider, September 30, 2024.
6. Larry and Catherine Pfaff, interview by Dan Schneider, October 4, 2024.
7. Malcolm Pike, interview by Dan Schneider, October 18, 2024.
8. Lynda Curnoe, email to Dan Schneider (and others), September 29, 2024.
9. Su Murdoch, note to Dan Schneider, September 30, 2024.
10. Dan Schneider, diary entry, June 23, 1990.
11. Larry Pfaff, "John Henry Clark House and Barn, 108 Robinson St. & 107 Ontario St. N., St. Marys—some architectural notes," n.d., 2. Email to authors, July 20, 2024.

CONCLUSION

1. This and the preceding quotation are from Su Murdoch, interview by Dan Schneider, October 1, 2024, and Julia Beck, letter to Lynne DiStefano, November 13, 1998, respectively.

INDEX

Note: Bold indicates an image caption.

Adamson, Anthony, 8, 13
Addington County, 34
Ainslie, H.F., 93, **95**
Albion Street cottages, Brantford, 52, **62**, 95
Alexander, George, 33
Alexander, Sir James Edward, **32**, **135**
Alwington Avenue cottage, Kingston, 93, **100**
Ancestral Roof: Domestic Architecture of Upper Canada (MacRae and Adamson), 8, 13
appeal of Ontario Cottages, 45, 53, 180
architectural pattern books, 69–79, 187n13
architectural styles, 45–52, 191n3
architecture, vernacular, 12, 186n4
asymmetry, 85, 187n14. *See also* symmetry
atlases, 32
Aylmer, 53, **66**
Ayr, **138**

Backwoods of Canada (Traill), 133
Bainbridge, Philip John, **126**
Bank Street North cottage, Millbrook, 135, **142**
Barber, William, 71
Barrie, 172
Barry Avenue cottage, Mississauga, 53, **64**
Bartell, Edmund, 73, **75**
Bayfield, 52, **60**
Beamsville, 94

Beck, Julia, 81
bedrooms, 156, 157, 160
Beech Street cottage, Collingwood, 53, **63**
Bejan, Adrian, 192n4
Belvedere, The, Port Hope, 95, **111**
Bengal huts, **133**, 134
bichromatic brickwork, 53
board-and-batten siding, 93, 94, 192n1
Bowmanville, 134, 137, **139**, **146**
Boyle, Richard, 46
Brant County, 33
Brantford, 32, 35, **42**, **43**, 52, **62**, 95
Brantford Cottage, 35
brick construction, 95
brick siding, 94, 95
Brighton Avenue cottage, Brantford, **42**
British American Cultivator, 94–95
British architecture, 45, 46
British Gothic architecture, 50
Britton, John, **35**
Broadway Street East cottage, Paris, 137, **150**
Brooklin, 160, **168**
Brunskill, Ronald William, 12, 186n5
Bungalow: The Production of a Global Culture (King), 131–132
bungalows, 15–16, **16**, 131, 187n14
Butler House, Niagara-on-the-Lake, 31–32, **36**, 159
By, Colonel John, **126**
Byng Avenue cottage, Cambridge, 134, **140**

Caledonia Street cottage, Stratford, 137, **153**
Cambridge, **17**, 52, **55**, 134, **140**, 159
Campbell, Colin, 46
Canada Farmer, 11, 51, **51**, 77, 78, 157, 186n1
Canadian Geographical Journal, 75
Carfrae Cottage, London, 52, **58**
Cassels Road East cottage, Brooklin, 160, **168**
Castle Frank (Simcoe), **50**
centre-hall plans, 155–157
chambers. *See* bedrooms
Charles Place, Kingston, 32, **38**, 96
Chinnery, George, **133**
Church Street cottage, Kitchener, 82, **82**, 84, 85, **87**, 137
clapboard siding, 93
Clapp–Palmer House, Consecon, 96, **112**, 124
classical architecture, 191n3
climate, design for, 133
cobblestones, 96
Cobourg, 134
Coffey, Brian, 93, 97
Colborne Lodge, Toronto, 97, **118**, 135, 190n22
Colborne Street cottage, London, **21**
Collingwood, 53, **63**
Commissariat Office, Fort Malden, 191n35
Commodore's Residence, Point Frederick, 191n35, 193n9
complementarity, 187n16
concrete, 97
Consecon, 96, 124
construction, 93, 95, 97, 124, **125**, 194n17
core characteristics of Ontario Cottages, 8–9, 12
Cornwall, 159, **159**, 163
Cottage built for my brother Killaly 4 miles from London (Simcoe), **15**
"cottage," as a term, 12–15
cottage orné, 15, **15**, 72–73, 189n12
cottage owners, 171–172
county maps and atlases, 32–35

Creek Cottage, Ayr, 134, **138**
Cruickston Farm, Cambridge, **17**
Curnoe, Greg, 173
Cutts, Anson Bailey, 75, 96

Davenport, Alan, 192n4
De architectura (Vitruvius), 46
Demorestville, 93, **99**
design for wind, 126
Designs for Agricultural Buildings Suited to Irish Estates (Taylor), 71–72, **72**
Designs for Cottages (Middleton), **73**
de Tuylls, Baron, 32, **32**
Diamond Cottage, 35
dining rooms, 157, 159
door and window placement, 84–86
Douro Street cottage, Stratford, 52, **61**
Downing, Andrew Jackson, 94, 136
drawing rooms, 157
Drew Cottage, Woodstock, 32, **40**, 137, **137**, 160, **160**
Drumsnab, Toronto, 32, 135, **135**
Dundas, 159
Dundas Street West cottage, Mississauga, **26**
Durham County, 33

Eastern Ontario, 95
Elgin County, 34
Eliot, George, 69, 70
Elizabethan architecture, 53
emigrant guides, 70, 75, 76, 79
Encyclopaedia of Cottage, Farm, and Villa Architecture and Furniture (Loudon), 69, 70, 74, 75, 76, 78, **79**
Ennals, Peter, 187n12
Essay on British Cottage Architecture (Malton), 45, 75
Essay on the Construction of Cottages Suited for the Dwellings of the Labouring Classes (Smith), 74

facades, symmetrical, 8, 12, 51
"Factors Affecting the Use of Construction
    Materials in Early Ontario" (Coffey), 93
Farm Buildings (Barber), 71
fieldstone, 96
five-bay cottages, 155
floor plans, 8–9, 155–161, **157**, **159**, **160**
*Folk Housing in Middle Virginia: A Structural
    Analysis of Historic Artifacts* (Glassie), 186n3
formality, 157
Fountain Street South cottage, Cambridge, 52, **55**
Fowler, Emerald D., 133, 134
framing, of hipped roof, 124, **125**
French doors, 85, 86
Frontenac County, 34

gables, 51, 123, 124–126, 188n12, 191n36
Gate Lodge, Ireland, **70**
Georgian period, 48–49, 50
Georgian style, 45
Gibbs, James, 81
Glasgow Street North cottage, Guelph, 137, **148**
Glassie, Henry, 186n3
God of Small Things (Roy), 131
Goderich, 32, **32**, **104**
golden ratio, 84, 85–86, 192n4
Gothic architecture, 50–51, **51**, **77**
Gothic Revival, 94, 188n13, 188n14
Government House, York, 191n35
Grafton, 134
granite, 96
Greek classical architecture, 51–52
Grenville County, 34
Guelph, **28**, 82, **82**, 84, **89**, 137, **148**
Gulliver's Travels (Swift), 123

Hamilton Place, Paris, 96, **120**
Hastings County, 34
heritage designation, 178, 181

hierarchy, 157, 160
High Victorian Gothic, 52, 53
hillsides, 176
*Hints for Picturesque Improvements in Ornamental
    Cottages, and Their Scenery* (Bartell), 73, **75**
history of Ontario Cottages, 9, 11–15, 31–35, 45–49,
    69–79
Holdsworth, Deryck W., 187n12
*Homeplace: The Making of the Canadian Dwelling
    over Three Centuries* (Ennals and Holdsworth),
    187n12
Hooey Cottage, Port Hope, 82, **82**, 84, 85, **88**, 97
House on the Thames (Ainslie), 93
housing, affordable, 35
housing categories, 12–13, 35
Howard, John George, 15, 75, 135, 155–156
H.R. Place, West Oxford, 156, **157**
Hunt, John Powell, **124**
Huron County, 34, **35**

*I quattro libri dell'architectura (The Four Books
    of Architecture)* (Palladio), 47
*Idea of the Cottage in English Architecture,
    The: 1760–1869* (Maudlin), 187n11
Illustrated Handbook of Vernacular Architecture
    (Brunskill), 186n5
impressions of the Ontario Cottage, 171–175, 180
India, 15, 131–132
Inverarden, Cornwall, 159, **159**, 160, **163**
Ireland, **70**, 71
Italianate style, 52

James Lazier House, Prince Edward
    County, **18–19**
James Street cottage, Kingston, **24**
James Street cottage, Stratford, 95, **110**
Johnson Cottage, Port Bruce, **20**
Jones, Inigo, 46

Kempenfelt Bay, 176
King, Anthony D., 131–132
Kingston, **24**, 32, **38**, 93, 96, **100**
King Street West cottage, Colborne, 123, **127**
Kirkland Street cottage, Guelph, **28**
kitchen ells, 159
Kitchener, 82, **82**, 84, **87**
kitchens, 159–160
Knight family, 137, **137**

labour, skilled, 97
L'Acadie (Alexander), **135**
Lamond, Robert, **49**, 75, 76, **77**, 191*n*27
Larkin Farms, Niagara-on-the-Lake, 97
Leeds County, 34
Lennox County, 34
limestone, 95, 96
Lincoln County, 33, 34
living rooms, 157
lodges, 189*n*3
log cabins, 96
log construction, 93, 96
London, 32, 52, **58**, 95, **108**
London Advertiser, 35
London Free Press, 95
Lonsdale, 124, **128**, **129**
Looking for Old Ontario: Two Centuries of Landscape Change (McIlwraith), 13
Loudon, J.C., 53, 69, 74, 75, 76–78, **79**, 190*n*17, 191*n*27, 191*n*30
Lovers Lane cottage, Bowmanville, 137, **146**
Lower Bytown (Bainbridge), **126**

MacRae, Marion, 8, 13
Magrath, Thomas William, 136
Main Street cottage, Newburgh, 160, **169**
Main Street cottage, Odessa, 135, **144**, **145**
Main Street North cottage, Bayfield, 52, **60**
Mallory Cottage, Haldimand, 134, **134**

Malton, James, 45, 75
Maple Cottage (Hunt), **124**
maps, 32, 33, 34
Marysville, **25**
Marysville Road cottage, Lonsdale, 124, **128**, **129**
Maudlin, Daniel, 187*n*11
McDougall Cottage, Cambridge, 96, 159, **159**, **164**, **165**
McIlwraith, Thomas F., 13
McLeod, Wm. C., 33
Middle Ages, 50, 52
Middlemarch (Eliot), 69, 70
Middlesex County, 33
Middlesex Prototype (1854), 155
Middleton, Charles, 72–73, **73**
Millbrook, 135, **142**
Minhinnick, Jeanne, 193*n*12
Mississauga, **26**, 53, **64**
Mitchell, **103**
Mornington Street cottage, Stratford, 53, **65**
Mud Cottage, The, Sparta, 93, **98**
Murdoch, Harry, 172
Murdoch, Su, 171, 172, 173–174, 176

Narrative of the Rise & Progress of Emigration, from the Counties of Lanark & Renfrew, to the New Settlements in Upper Canada, on Government Grant (Lamond), **49**, 75, 76, **77**
Nathaniel Reid Cottage, London, 95, **108**
neighbours, 174–175
neoclassicism, 49
Newburgh, 160, **169**
Niagara Escarpment, 95, 96
Niagara-on-the-Lake, **27**, 31, **36**, 94, 97, **121**, 159
Niagara River Parkway cottage, Niagara-on-the-Lake, **121**
Norfolk, 33

Normandale, 82, **82**, **90**, 124
Norris, Darrell A., 12

occupants of Ontario Cottages, 171–178
Odessa, 135, **144**, **145**
Ontario County, 34
Ontario Heritage Act, 181
Oxford County, 33

Palladian style, 45, 46, **46**, 47, 48, **49**, 53
Palladio, Andrea, 45, 46, **46**, 47, 48, 81
Papworth, John Buonarotti, 132, 133
Paris, 96, **116**, **117**, **120**, 137, **150**
parlours, 157
pattern books, 69–79, 187n13
Peel County, 33, 34
Perry–Scroggie House, Guelph, 82, **82**, 84, 85, 86, **89**, 96
Perth County, 34
Picturesque and Architectural Views for Cottages, Farm Houses, and Country Villas (Middleton), 72
Picturesque Eclecticism, 52
Pilkington, Robert, 191n35
pitch, of roofs, 126, 135. *See also* roof, hipped
Plaw, John, 15, 16, **16**, 73, 132, 187n13
plinth, 131–132, 193n4
porches, 12. *See also* verandas
Port Hope, **23**, 32, 82, **82**, 84, **88**, 95, 97, 160, 173, **179**
porticos, 47, 48, **50**
Port Ryerse, **14**
preservation, 181
Prince Edward County, **18**, 34
proportions, 81–86, 172–173. *See also* golden ratio; symmetry
Prospect Cottage, Haldimand, 134, **134**
protection, feeling of, 123. *See also* impressions of the Ontario Cottage

Queen Anne Revival, 53
Queen Street cottage, Paris, 96, **116**, **117**

rain, design for, 126
Regency Cottages, 13, 49, **137**, 159, 189n11
Res. of John Britton, **35**
Ridout, Samuel, **136**
rivers, 176
Robert Youdan Terrace, Port Hope, 173, **179**
Rokewood, Woodstock, **41**, 135
Roman classical architecture, 45–46, 51–52
Romanesque Revival, 52
roof, gabled, 51, 123, 124–126, 188n12, 191n36
roof, hipped, 12, 13, 31–32, 34, 47, 96, 123–126, **125**, 174–175
Rose-Belford's Canadian Monthly and National Review (Fowler), 133
Rose Cottage, Oakville, **12**, 52, **56**
Rosedale, 32
Roselands, Toronto, **136**
Rowan House, Demorestville, 93, **99**
Roy, Arundhati, 131
Royal Engineers, 132, 191n35, 193n9
rural areas, 33–35, 175–176
Rural Residences (Papworth), 132, 133

Schneider, Dan, 171
Scotland, 74, 76, 78, 81
Scottish architecture, 73, 75, 76, 78, **79**, 96, 126, 190n17
seasons, 133, 159
Series of Plans for Cottages or Habitations of the Labourer (Wood), 71, **71**
servants, 156, 157
Settler's House on the Thames (Ainslie), **95**
shade, 133, 193n12
shape of Ontario Cottages, 155
siding, 93, 94, 95, 97, 192n1
Simcoe, Elizabeth, **15**, **50**

site elevation, 159–160
sitting rooms, 157
size, small, 172
Sketches for Country Houses, Villas and Rural Dwellings (Plaw), 15, **16**, 73, 132, 187n13
Small Gothic Cottage, 51, **51**, 52, 77–79, 82, **82**, 84, 85, 124, 157, **157**
smallness, 172
Smith, George, 74
Smith, James Avon, 78
Sparta, 93, **98**
St. Catherines, **29**
St. David Street cottage, Mitchell, **103**
stewardship, 177–178
St. Marys, 96, 159, **160**, **166**, 171, 172, 176
stone construction, 95, 96, 190n17
stories of cottages, 178
Stratford, 32, 52, 53, **61**, **65**, 95, 137, **153**
St. Thomas, 53, **67**
stucco siding, 97
suburbs, 35
summer cottages, **14**, **50**
Swift, Jonathan, 123
Swiss Cottage, Aylmer, 53, **66**
symmetry, 8, 12, 46, 85, 174. *See also* asymmetry; proportions

Taylor, Arthur C., 72, **72**
Templar Cottage, London, 95, **108**
Ten Books on Architecture (Vitruvius), 46
tenure in cottages, 177
Thatched Indian Hut with a Woman and Child and a Tethered Cow at the Entrance (Chinnery), **133**
Thomas, William, 79
three-bay cottages, 155
timber-frame construction, 93
tongue-and-groove siding, 93, 94
Toronto, 32, 95, 97, **118**, **136**
Traill, Catharine Parr, 133, 136

Tremaine, George, 32, 34
tympanums, 48

Unwin family, 136, **136**
Upper Canada, 31, 70, 74, 75, 95
Usher Street cottage, Brantford, **43**

Van Norman–Guiler Cottage, Normandale, 82, **82**, 84, 85, 86, **90**, 124
Vansittart Avenue cottage, Woodstock, **22**
verandas, 12, 15, **16**, 32, 131–137, 175–176, 193n2, 194n17
vernacular architecture, 186n4
Villa Emo, **46**
Vitruvius, 46, 81, 123

Waltham Cottage, Bowmanville, 134, **139**
Warner Road cottage, Niagara-on-the-Lake, **27**
weather, design for, 126, 133
Welland County, 33, 34
Wellington Street South cottage, Goderich, **104**
Wells, Camille, 186n3
West Oxford, 156, **157**
Whalen Road cottage, Marysville, **25**
White, Randall, 31
Wilczek, Frank, 187n16
Wilderness, Niagara-on-the-Lake, 94, **106**
William Trick Cottage, Port Hope, **23**
wind, design for, 126, 192n4
windows, 84, 85, 175, 176
Windrush Cottage, St. Marys, 159, **160**, **166**, 172
Wood, John, 71, **71**, 189n6
Woodale, Dundas, 159, **162**
Woodburn, Beamsville, 94, **107**, 159
Wood–Simpson House, St. Marys, 96, **115**, 160
Woodstock, **22**, 32, 33, **40**, **41**, 135, 137, **137**, 160, **160**

Yates Street cottage, St. Catherines, **29**